Texas Blue Ribbon Fly-Fishing

DIANE HICKS

Danny Hicks

Texas Fly-Fishing Guide

CAPTIAN SCOTT SPARROW

CAPTIAN SCOTT SPARROW

Danny Hicks

Frank
Amato
PORTLAND

Acknowledgments

Thanks to my friends, Steve O'Neill and Katherine Danie, Kathy and Scott Sparrow of Kingfisher Inn, Tony Sahyoun of Holiday Inn Town Lake, in Austin, Kenny and Mary McDaniel of Shady Glade Resort at Caddo Lake, Raye Carrington and David Jones at Raye Carrington on the Llano River, Redfish Lodge on Copano Bay, Duel Glass, Tarpon Inn in Port Aransas, Best Western Sonora Inn, The Gruene Mansion Inn, and the Best Western Rose Garden in Brownsville for their generous hospitality.

Thanks to guides Robert C. Woodruff, Bill Higdon, Alvin Dedeaux, Johnny Quiroz II, Marcus Rodriguez, Andy Morreau, Kelly Watson, Dean Heffner, and Gerald Bailey, Captains Kathy and Scott Sparrow, Eric Glass, Bill Smith, and Paul Brown for fishing with me. Thanks to Joey Lin, and all the guides, captains, and Texas Parks and Wildlife biologists for their expertise and facts, to Katy Mitchell of Bass Pro Shops, Pat Lytle and Tony Tekansik, of Pentax Imaging Company, John Mazurkiewicz of Catalyst Marketing and Scientific Anglers, Eric Kraimer of Red Heron Sales and Marketing and Simms Fishing Products, Thomas and Thomas Rod Makers, and Galvan Fly Reels for their assistance, Bass Pro Shops' Offshore Angler, Chris Jackson of Action Angler, Scott Sparrow, Robert C. Woodruff, Tony Accardo of Accardo Tackle Company, and Larry Haines of The Shop, for providing flies for pictures. Special thanks to my wife Diane for modeling, holding fish, taking pictures for me while on her birding excursions, and always being supportive.

Frank Amato Publications, Inc.
P.O. Box 82112, Portland, Oregon 97282
503.653.8108 • www.amatobooks.com

Photographs by the author unless otherwise noted.

Book and Cover Design: Kathy Johnson
Map Illustrations: Kathy Johnson

Printed in Hong Kong
ISBN-13: 978-1-57188-430-5
UPC: 0-81127-00264-1

1 3 5 7 9 10 8 6 4 2

Contents

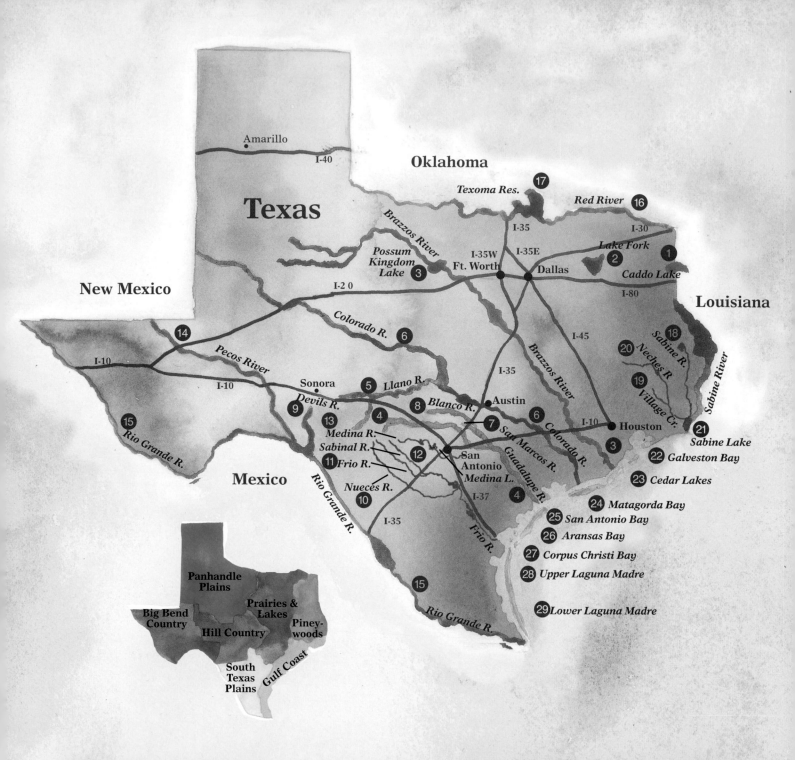

Amarillo

I-40

Oklahoma

Texas

New Mexico

Louisiana

Texoma Res. ⑰

Red River ⑯

I-35

I-30

Brazzos River

Possum Kingdom Lake ③

I-35W
Ft. Worth

I-35E
Dallas

Lake Fork ②

①

Caddo Lake

I-80

I-2 0

Colorado R. ⑥

I-10

⑭

Pecos River

I-45

Brazzos River

⑱ *Sabine R.*

Sabine River

I-10

Sonora

⑤ *Llano R.*

Devils R. ⑨

I-35

⑳ *Neches R*

⑲ *Village Cr.*

⑧ *Blanco R.* Austin

⑥ *Colorado R.*

③ Houston ㉑

Sabine Lake

⑬ *Medina R.*

④

San Marcos R.

I-10

㉒ *Galveston Bay*

⑮

Rio Grande R.

Sabinal R.

⑪ *Frio R.*

⑫

San Antonio

Medina L.

Guadalupe R.

㉓ *Cedar Lakes*

Mexico

Nueces R.

⑩

I-37

④

㉔ *Matagorda Bay*

Rio Grande R.

I-35

㉕ *San Antonio Bay*

㉖ *Aransas Bay*

㉗ *Corpus Christi Bay*

⑮

Frio R.

㉘ *Upper Laguna Madre*

Rio Grande R.

㉙ *Lower Laguna Madre*

Panhandle Plains

Big Bend Country

Prairies & Lakes

Hill Country

Piney-woods

South Texas Plains

Gulf Coast

Lady Bird Lake and downtown Austin.

McKitterick Canyon in Guadalupe National Park.

Texas Bluebonnets.

Running along Caddo Lake's "Government Ditch."

Brazos River.

Introduction

Few people think of water when they think of Texas. Even in this age of information, the perception of Texas as a dusty land that only cowboys and rattlesnakes can love, remains firmly fixed. Not that this perception is false, a big part of Texas matches that concept, but a bigger part does not.

Water is a precious commodity in Texas, especially out west. Average annual precipitation varies from above 54 inches to less than 14 inches in more or less vertical bands from east to west. Ferocious storms produce intense rain (it can't rain harder anywhere than it does in Texas) throughout the state, but most of that water quickly, and dangerously, runs off in the form of killer flash floods. This "feast or famine" rain scenario makes Texas a reservoir-dependent state. Without them, there would be few dependable sources of surface water for drinking and irrigation—certainly nowhere near what the present population demands. By volume, the 212 reservoirs provide the majority of freshwater angling opportunities in Texas.

Texas reservoirs are rightly famous for big largemouth bass, and offer a chance of catching a 10-pound largemouth on a fly. Fifty-two of the state's public reservoirs have produced largemouth bass in excess of 13 pounds. Texas reservoirs also hold native northern largemouth, and many have spotted, white (called sand bass in northern Texas), striped, and hybrid bass. Some of the deeper and clearer reservoirs in north and central Texas have non-native smallmouth bass. Big sunfish, including redear, aka "shellcrackers," that routinely exceed a pound and can approach three pounds in Texas, and a host of other sunfish species, also live in Texas reservoirs along with catfish and rough fish that readily take flies.

Northern largemouth and Guadalupe bass are native to the clear, spring-fed streams of the Texas Hill Country, but not all are pure strain. Northern largemouth have mixed with Florida bass to a large extent, and Guadalupe bass readily hybridize with smallmouth bass. Texas rivers and streams may hold northern, northern/Florida hybrids, spotted, Guadalupe, Guadalupe/smallmouth hybrids, and smallmouth bass, or any combination of these species, plus a wide assortment of sunfish, catfish and rough fish like that of the reservoirs.

On the vast, barrier island sheltered Texas flats, you can stalk red drum, seatrout, southern flounder, and black drum, to name a few. In the bays' deeper water, off jetties, near passes, and in the surf, there are tarpon, snook, jack crevalle, and dozens of incidental species that are possibilities. Beyond the surf line (usually), and far out in the Gulf, you can catch groupers, barracuda, tuna, sharks, and billfish along with many of the other species that live in the Gulf of Mexico.

Seatrout hooked in Intracoastal Waterway while wading the adjoining flats. Anglers must watch their step, the drop-off is sharp.

Texas Regions

There is so much area and physical contrast in Texas that writing accurately about the state as a whole is an exercise in futility. You can say that Texas is big, and the people tend to be friendly, but without qualifiers, that is it. Even saying that the summers are hot, and the winters are mild to warm, has to be qualified a little. Panhandle and west Texas winters are more like those of New Mexico, which are not mild, and summer temperatures in the western mountains are somewhat moderated by altitude and low humidity which allows the temperature to drop at night. Prevailing onshore winds keep the coast semi-comfortable in the summer heat. With water temperatures in the 80s and air temperatures even hotter, the wind is not cool like a Pacific sea breeze, but when it stops you will notice, and, begin to sweat.

To address this lack of uniformity, Texas is often divided into regions, each of which has a degree of geographical and climatic consistency. The standard division, used by state agencies including the Texas Parks and Wildlife Department (TPWD), separates the state into seven regions.

The far western portion, which inspired and most resembles the prevailing cowboy, cactus, and dust stereotype, is called the Big Bend Country, for the Rio Grande's southern loop and its associated national park. Guadalupe Mountains National Park, and 8,749-foot Guadalupe Peak, the highest point in the Texas' Trans-Pecos Range, shares a border with New Mexico. This part of Texas also includes the Chihuauan Desert, vast oil fields, and plenty of wide-open spaces.

Immediately east of Big Bend Country is the Texas Hill Country, with its limestone bedrock and rocky cedar-covered hills—the proverbial heart of Texas. Swift, spring-fed streams lined with bald cypress make this part of Texas highly attractive to fly-fishermen.

Above: A subdivision lake in the Dallas-Ft. Worth Metroplex.

Above left: Fall color in Guadalupe Mountains National Park

Lower: Vulture roost at Possum Kingdom's Morris Sheppard Dam.

Facing page: Casting a popper to the shoreline of a private east Texas lake.

COOKIE BALLOU

East and north of the Hill Country is the Prairies and Lakes section. This area of farms, ranches, and prairie is where east meets west, includes the Dallas Fort Worth Metroplex, and at least 50 major reservoirs.

The Panhandle Plains in far north Texas are described as "gloriously flat," but despite its level reputation there is a spectacular canyon south of Amarillo called Palo Duro. The canyon is 120 miles long and more than 1000 feet deep in places. The famous nature artist Georgia O'Keefe painted it many times when she worked as a teacher in Amarillo and later in nearby Canyon. Farther south, amid rolling hills, low buttes and rock bluffs is the upper Brazos River and its uppermost impoundment Possum Kingdom Lake—the clearest lake in Texas.

The far eastern part of Texas is known as Piney Woods. It has alligators, swamps, bayous, and Texas' only naturally formed lake, Caddo. Lowlands are dominated by bald cypress trees draped in Spanish moss, and the highlands by pines.

The South Texas Plains are essentially all the land from San Antonio to the south, except for the coast. This region includes the fertile Rio Grande Valley and a vast brushy region of flat land and low trees. It is quite wild. The Rio Grande forms its southern border from north of Eagle Pass almost to the Harlingen—Brownsville area where the coast region begins.

The Gulf Coast region runs from Boca Chica Beach at the Mexican border to the Louisiana side of Sabine Lake, and inland to include the coastal flats and the Houston metro area. It is an extremely flat region where there are shallow bays, salt and brackish marshes, barrier island beaches, and the Gulf of Mexico. The upper portion is temperate in climate and foliage, and the lower sub-tropical.

11

Trespassing in Texas

Unlike some parts of the country, trespassing is not tolerated as a kind of "good ole boy" tradition in Texas. Quite the opposite, private property rights are ingrained in Texans and Texas law. The Republic of Texas sold most of its public land to repay Mexican War debt, and with the exception of the state parks, two national parks, a national seashore, four national forests, and a modest amount of additional government land, fishing in Texas is done on or adjacent to private land.

Water in streams, navigable or not, is public property, but you have no right to cross private property to access a stream or to get out of one, and it is illegal to drive in a stream bed. You can access private land above the high-water mark only to scout and portage obstructions, and landowners cannot obstruct the public's right of way within the stream with fences or other barriers. Texas trespassing laws are intricate and intriguing. Some date back to the days of the Republic and even to the time of Spanish conquistadors.

Typical of crossings in developed areas, this bridge over the Blanco River is "drop off" access only.
If you are confused, about what you can and can't do here,
the signs spell it out.

Bill Higdon drifts a nymph at the base of "Devil's Playground Rapids."
Sign or no sign, riverside property is private and you are expected
to stay in the river and off the bank.

Discussing the particulars of Texas trespassing law is a worthy intellectual exercise, but landowners seldom care to mince words with intruders, and be assured that law-enforcement officers will side with the landowner in all but the most extreme instances. Stories about bullets being fired at people are widespread, especially in west Texas where some property owners still refuse to accept that people have a right to be in "their" rivers.

Access is an essential part of fishing in Texas, streams in particular. What you can do and where you can go depends on where you can get in and out of a stream. Most floaters do day trips, and certain stream sections are isolated because public accesses are more than a day's float apart. If gravel bars and islands within the high-water marks are scarce, the lack of legal camping sites further guarantees isolation. While dealing with private property along streams adds a degree of difficulty to Texas fishing, it also impedes casual river usage and that reduces trash and illegal fishing. Texas' ocean beaches (not bay shores) are public, but as with streams, you must access them lawfully.

This book does not dwell on accesses, which constantly change, thereby presenting the risk of erroneous information. Local contacts are the best source for up-to-date and factual access information.

Texas Freshwater Fish

Largemouth Bass

By far the most popular freshwater fish in Texas, largemouth bass are found throughout the state in reservoirs, rivers, streams and private ponds, or tanks (short for stock tanks used for cattle watering) as they are often called in Texas. Northern largemouth are native to Texas, but Florid-strain largemouths, which grow larger, have been introduced into most of the state's reservoirs. Ten-pound northern largemouths are rare, but Florida fish routinely reach that size and can exceed 20 pounds. Florida bass have been stocked in Texas reservoirs since the early 70s, and fish that are all or part Florida strain have accounted for all Texas-size records. The largest, and current state record, is an 18.18-pounder from Lake Fork, and the state fly-fishing record is 14.14. That fish was caught on a popper in 2000 from the Meredith Stilling Basin on the Canadian River in the Panhandle north of Amarillo.

Fly-fishing guide Rob Woodruff with an "average" good Lake Fork bass.

Before Florida-strain fish were introduced to Texas, the state largemouth record was a 13.5-pound fish caught in 1943 from Medina Lake near San Antonio. With modern DNA technology and a scale, that fish was determined to have Florida genes, according to David Campbell of the Texas Freshwater Fisheries Center. The mystery includes an undocumented story of a truck carrying bass from Florida to the King Ranch in the 20s or 30s that experienced problems and was forced to release its load in the only available reservoir—Medina which was impounded in 1913. Why a truck with problems could make it to Medina and not the King Ranch is unclear, but it is a fact that Florida was known to export its native bass in those days, and it is possible that big bass from other areas of the country were also of that strain. In more recent history, it is said that Bob Kemp who eventually became the TPWD's executive director made an unofficial trip to Florida in the early 70s and secretly brought them back to Texas.

Florida bass are essentially reservoir fish, and the northern largemouths remain the principal large-river bass in Texas. In current, large northerns are beautifully streamlined and highly prized. Four- and five-pounders are common in Texas streams but difficult to hook and even more difficult to land. In larger rivers with big pools and good habitat, some may approach twice that size, however these big river bass are likely to have Florida genes.

Guadalupe Bass

Guadalupe bass are the official Texas State fish, and are found only in Texas. They are loved by anglers, especially fly-fishermen, because of their delightful propensity to hold and feed in fast water. The shallowest and fastest riffles usually hold smaller Guadalupes, but no matter their size, all "guads" love current. They are sometimes referred to as "Texas brook trout," but their affinity for swift water is more like that of rainbow trout than brookies.

Guadalupes are native to the northern and eastern Edwards Plateau (Texas Hill Country) river drainages including the Brazos, Colorado, Guadalupe, and San Antonio rivers. They are also native to the lower Colorado which is east of the Edwards Plateau, but

Guadalupe bass.

are not so numerous as in other parts of their range. Guadalupes can weigh over three pounds, but most are around 10 inches.

Smallmouth Bass

Smallmouth have been introduced into several reservoirs and many Texas streams. Most were stocked in the Hill Country during the 70s, the thinking was that the larger smallmouth would provide good sport. It seemed like a good idea, until it became apparent that smallmouth were hybridizing with Guadalupes and that the Guadalupes were in danger of being hybridized out of existence.

Clear rocky reservoirs such as Lake Meredith on the Canadian River in the Panhandle and Whitney on the Brazos River and the Devils River are premier smallmouth fisheries.

Smallmouth/Guadalupe Hybrids

Bass in streams that hold Guadalupes and smallmouth bass are hybrids, pure Guadalupes and smallmouth have either ceased to exist or become rare. It is estimated that only 30% of Guadalupe bass are pure. Some bass look more like one than the other, but to identify one as a pure Guadalupe or smallmouth would

Smallmouth Guadalupe hybrid.

be questionable. To be certain a bass is a pure Guadalupe you would have to catch it in a river such as the Llano where smallmouth have never been stocked.

Guadalupe/smallmouth hybrids are handsome fish, but they are not so well adapted to the flood and drought Texas river cycles as pure Guadalupes or the northern largemouth. Hybrids are known to occasionally hybridize with native largemouths, producing weak offspring, and fisheries biologists wish to avoid this. Smallmouth stocking has been discontinued throughout the Guadalupe's range.

Spotted Bass

Spotted bass are native to east Texas and coastal plains streams and rivers from the Red to the Guadalupe river systems, but not in the Edwards Plateau. Rivers that run through the Hill Country and to the coast usually have native spotted bass in their lower reaches, Guadalupes in the upper portions, and both where the rivers transition from Hill Country to coastal plain. Spotted bass and Guadalupes do not hybridize.

Spotted bass are heavy for their size and fight hard, but rarely exceed five pounds in Texas. Sometimes called Kentucky bass, because they were first identified as a distinct species in Kentucky's Kentucky Lake, spots hold in faster current than largemouths and do well in water that is too turbid for smallmouth. Some have been introduced into lakes in other parts of Texas. Alabama has another subspecies of spotted bass, and they have been introduced to the upper Colorado River.

Sea Bass

Sometimes referred to as temperate or true bass, Texas has white, striped, white/striped hybrids, yellow bass, and yellow/white bass hybrids. White bass live in most Texas lakes and run up rivers and creeks each spring to spawn. They are aggressive, strong, and fun to catch with fly equipment. Most weigh about a pound, but five-pounders have been caught in Texas. Big white bass are females, which run later than the smaller males. White bass are native to the Mississippi and Great Lakes drainage, but not Texas. They first appeared in Caddo Lake, and then were spread across the state with authorized and unauthorized stockings.

Striped bass native to the east coast have been put into many Texas lakes. As with white bass, stripers must have running water in which to spawn successfully. Most of these lakes must be maintained with hatchery fish, but Texoma has a self-sustaining population. Stripers are thrilling to catch on a fly, and can exceed fifty pounds in Texas.

White/striped bass hybrids are a hatchery product, although a few occur naturally. They are more aggres-

Yellow bass.

sive than stripers, and much bigger than white bass. They can attain a weight of twenty pounds or more. Hybrids are shorter and thicker than striped bass and are extremely strong.

Yellow bass look much like white bass, but are more cylindrical, smaller, and of course, yellow. The state record is less than a pound and a half, but a four-pound white/yellow hybrid was caught at Lake Fork in 2003.

Sunfish/Panfish

Sunfish are usually called "brim" in east Texas, and "perch" throughout the rest of the state. Of course they are neither. Brim is apparently derived from bream, a

Bluegill

European rough fish that, to my knowledge, does not exist in the United States. Texas does have some walleye and a few yellow perch, but that is it for real perch. Sunfish and panfish are everywhere in Texas. You can catch them in riffles, lakes, and muddy backwaters. Some are quite large. Recently a 2.63-pound redear sunfish, was caught (and released) in Lady Bird Lake, a reservoir on the Colorado River, in Austin. Not only was the fish not a state record, it wasn't a lake record. The Texas record redear was caught there in 1997, it weighed 2.99 pounds. There are official state records for bluegill, spotted, green, hybrid, redbreast (an introduced species sometimes called yellow bellies), longear, and orange breast sunfish.

George Assenheimer with monster crappie caught on a spinner-fly.

Texas has both black and white crappie, rock, warmouth, and Rio Grande perch, the northernmost species of cichlids, a family of tropical fish.

Texas Trout

When one speaks of trout in Texas, they are generally speaking of seatrout. Freshwater trout fishing in the Lone Star State is limited, and mostly of the seasonal va-

Stream bred McCloud rainbow in McKittrick Creek.

riety. TPWD stocks trout in urban ponds, impoundments, state parks, and tailwaters around the state in winter, and most go home with anglers shortly thereafter.

On cool wet years, a few trout carryover in the Brazos River downstream of Possum Kingdom Lake, and they are known to survive year round in the 65-foot-deep Meredith Stilling Basin, below Meredith Lake on the Canadian River in the Panhandle. Canyon Lake Tailwater on the Guadalupe River is Texas' only significant year-round trout stream.

McKittrick Creek, in Guadalupe Mountains National Park, has McCloud rainbows, but fishing is not allowed. McKittrick is the only naturally cold trout stream in Texas and could have been a cutthroat stream at one time—but that is considered doubtful—the creek is isolated from other trout populations. According to Wallace Pratt, a local rancher, there were no fish whatsoever in the creek prior to stocking.

Trout were stocked in 1927 by J.C. Hunter who owned the Frijole Ranch, which is now part of the park. McCloud rainbows can be over ten pounds, but according to park ranger Cookie Ballou, six inches is about as big as they get in McKittrick Creek. Sunfish and black bass were also stocked by the ranchers. The bass promptly disappeared, but the sunfish survived in limited numbers, along with the trout.

Other Species

Chain pickerel

Both chain and grass pickerel are native to east Texas, but grass pickerel are not large enough to warrant much interest—the state record is less than half a pound. Chain pickerel grow to nearly five pounds, and take flies aggressively. Texas has blue, channel, and flathead catfish. The one-time world-record 121.5-pound blue catfish was caught in Lake Texoma in 2004 and now lives under the name of "Splash" in the Texas Freshwater Fisheries Center in Athens. Flathead and channel catfish in the clear Hill Country streams and lakes take flies readily. Kelly Watson, a Hill Country guide and outfitter, says that catfish can't make it by grubbing along the bottom like they do in big muddy rivers, and are forced to sight-feed and chase prey.

Rough fish are popular with fly-fishermen in Texas. Spotted gar, carp, and buffalo, among others, are all catchable with flies. In east Texas you can catch bowfin.

Reservoirs & Lakes

Above: Dick and Charlie's Tea Room, a former "speakeasy" near Uncertain, Texas, on Caddo Lake.
Top right: Lake Whitney Dam.

Classic bayou boat on Caddo Lake.
Left: Fishing along a boat trail on Caddo Lake.
Above: Stocker striper.

Caddo Lake

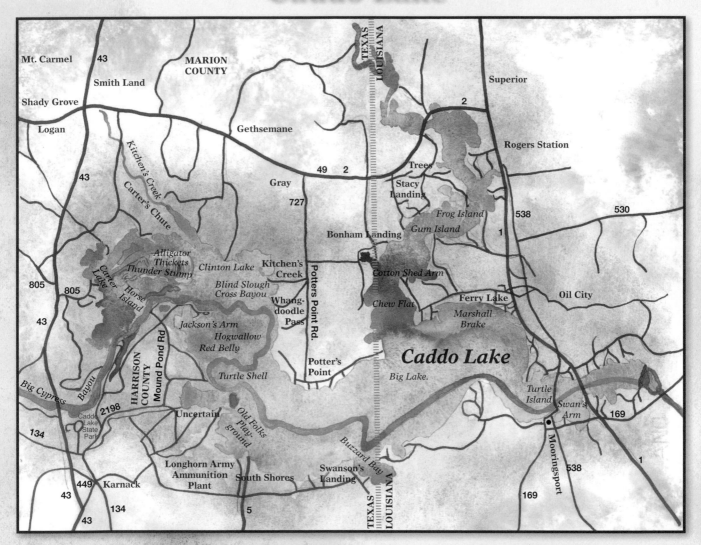

Named for the Caddo Indians, one of a culturally advanced group of tribes that lived in permanent housing and grew crops in addition to hunting deer, bison, and bear. The Caddos gave Texas its name—derived from "tejas"—their word for friend.

The best fishing and scenery on Caddo is from mid to late spring. Largemouth bass are the main attraction. Caddo largemouths are pretty fish, with distinctive markings and a dark green coloration to match the luxuriant vegetation. Caddo bass feed primarily on small sunfish, but shad are also an important food source. Frogs, insects, crawfish, small snakes and anything else they can capture round out their diet.

Caddo also has spotted, white, yellow, and hybrid striped bass. Chain pickerel are plentiful and fun to catch with flies. Caddo holds both black and white crappie (called "sac-a-lait" in those parts), and crappie fishing is quite popular there, especially in winter. A variety of sunfish, including redear and bluegill that can go a pound or better, all three catfish species, numerous rough fish that may take a fly, and bowfin are all possibilities at Caddo.

Caddo is sometimes identified as the only natural lake in Texas. While it was initially formed naturally by a log jam, (in Indian legend, a massive earthquake, possibly the New Madrid caused it), it is now a reservoir. The log jam, known as the Red River Raft that lodged near Shreveport, Louisiana, was approximately 100 miles long, and backed water from the Red River upstream and into Big Cypress Bayou, flooding a swamp that became Caddo Lake. The jam was broken in 1874, to reopen shipping between Shreveport and New Orleans. Once the jam was removed, Caddo drained, and the area reverted back to a swamp.

Steamboats could no longer reach the upstream cities of Jefferson, and the notorious Port Caddo which was the designated customs port of entry for the area. Port Caddo's notoriety stemmed from the town's steadfast refusal to remit port taxes to the Republic of Texas. When Mirabeau Lamar, the Republic's second president, sent the Harrison County Sheriff to collect port taxes, the townspeople killed the sheriff and burned his tax rolls in the street. The tax rebellion was quelled when Texas was admitted to the union and Port Caddo lost its "port of entry" status.

It was the discovery of oil that brought the lake back. The world's first over-water oil well was constructed at Caddo in 1911 by the Gulf Refining Company, (which became Gulf Oil Company), and many of the same techniques that were first used at Caddo, are still in use today. Moving heavy drilling equipment through the swamp proved impossible, so the oil companies persuaded the Corps of Engineers, who had previously financed the destruction of the jam, to build a long earthen dam in Louisiana to re-flood the lake. The dam was built in 1914, and was restored in 1971.

Caddo is less of a lake than a wetland, punctuated by named lakes, brakes, arms, bays, sloughs, ditches, the bayou's channel, and numerous areas with folksy names like Red Belly, Hog Wallow, and Old Folks Playground. Boat trails wind through the swamp. Some are ditches that have been dug by the WPA, or slaves, some are creek channels, and others have been washed out to a navigable depth by boat traffic. Though the main routes are marked like roads, Caddo is as easy a place to get turned around as there is. If you stay in the main areas and around other fishermen, you will be fine, but if you go into the backwaters and away from the marked boat roads, getting lost is a distinct possibility. Fishermen have done so and consequently spent the night in the swamp, and you could do the same. Even locals occasionally get turned around when concentrating on fishing rather that where they are going. A guide is highly recommend on Caddo if you want to see and fish more than a small area of the lake, or get into some back areas.

Officially 26,810 acres at Conservation Pool, that figure contains uncountable islands that may or may not be inundated depending on the lake's level which varies 4 to 8 feet. Caddo's average depth is 9 feet with a maximum of 20, and there is a great deal of one- to three-foot water. Cover in the form of submerged and emergent vegetation, including several species of water lilies, grass, and exotics like hydrilla, covers at least 60 percent of the lake. Fallen logs, brush, and cypress trees are everywhere. Boat mobility is increasingly limited as the year progresses and the vegetation grows, until it begins to die back in fall.

Spring floods once kept Caddo's vegetation in check, by flushing excessive vegetation, silt, and nutrients out of the lake and keeping its level high so there was less area for vegetation to start. Since Lake O' the Pines was impounded upstream on Big Cypress Creek in 1959 (same watercourse, but it is called a creek up there), the floods have been tempered, and weed growth has increased dramatically. Caddo's other major tributaries, Little Cypress, and Black Cypress creeks still bring floodwaters, but with Big Cypress Bayou tamed it is not enough to effectively retard weed growth.

When the sun goes down the vegetation depletes oxygen from the lake. Mike Ryan, the local biologist, says that 50% of Texas' portion of the lake, which is shallower and less open than the Louisiana part, has an oxygen level less than one part per million (ppm) during summer. Fish need about six ppm to be healthy, so a great deal of the shallow weedy water in Caddo that looks fishy, is not, when weed growth is at its peak. Fish kills are uncommon because fish move out of the shallow low-oxygen backwaters, to deeper, more open areas with better oxygen levels. Carter's and Clinton lakes, Turtle Shell, Hogwallow, Red Belly, and Jackson's Arm on the upper lake are overgrown with weeds and likely to be low on oxygen during summer. Once depleted, the oxygen level is these areas is unlikely to increase sufficiently till mid to late November. Open, deep, or moving water, and near by shallows, from the town of Uncertain to the dam in Louisiana will hold fish all year. Summer is tough, but if you stick to oxygenated areas you can catch fish. In winter, the vegetation goes dormant or dies back, and Caddo has been described as having a ghostly feel, especially in the backwaters. In spring, this condition rapidly reverses with vegetation beginning to grow, and the fish becoming active.

Largemouth in Caddo tend to grow slowly for the first two years of their lives, but make up the difference in later years. The lake's 14- to 18-inch slot limit, allows anglers to take smaller bass and reduce the competition.

As with most Texas lakes, the largemouths in Caddo are all or part Florida bass. Before the Florida strain was introduced in the early 80s, a big bass at Caddo was six pounds. In the late 80s after the Florida fish had a chance to grow, the lake record was broken repeatedly until a lake-record 16-pounder was caught in 1992. That fish was donated to the ShareLunker Program. Funded by Budweiser, the Program borrows largemouths of 13 pounds or larger from anglers and uses them for spawning and research programs to improve the genes of largemouth bass stocked in Texas. The program runs from October 15th to April 30th. Before October and after April, the Texas heat puts bass at risk of not surviving the necessary handling and transportation. After spawning, bass are returned to the angler for release or can be donated permanently. The big Caddo bass was released back where it was caught. The exact location is a secret, but it was in the Big Lake area.

Releasing big bass at Caddo is also encouraged by Bass Life Associates, a privately funded sportsman's group. Bass Life sponsors an incentive program that offers anglers who catch and release a largemouth of 8 pounds or more, a deal on fiberglass replicas—the bigger the fish, the better the deal. Bass Life's, Trophy Replica Program will pay 50% of the replica's cost for fish up to 8.9 pounds, 75% on bass 9 to 9.9 pounds, and 100% for 10-pound or bigger largemouth that are weighed at one of two local marinas and released alive at those marinas. Bass Life Associates also helps renovate Caddo's boat road markers, and sponsors fishing events for kids.

The trophy program provides TPWD with information about Caddo's big bass. Of 176 entries over a three-year period, 23 were recaptured once, and four twice. Only 15% were pure Florida strain, 45% were first-generation Florida-northern hybrids, and 40% were second or more generation hybrids. There were no pure northerns. No bass were recaptured near the marinas, and six were caught within a half mile of where they were first caught. Eighty-five percent of the big bass were caught in the lake's middle section where the best combination of structure, habitat, and water quality exists.

Kenny McDaniel with a handsome Caddo largemouth.

Caddo's combination of shallow water and abundant weedy and woody structure is ideal for fly-fishing. Despite this, Kenny McDaniel, who guides on the lake, and with his wife Mary, owns Shady Glade Resort in Uncertain, says that you can go months without seeing a fly-fisherman at Caddo. Kenny did not fly-fish when we first met, but the next time I saw him he did. In the interim, Kenny had gone to Wal-Mart and spent $26 on a complete fly outfit, including flies. His first day fly-fishing yielded nine bass, up to five pounds 10 ounces, and an undetermined number of sunfish. Kenny's knowledge of the lake played a big part in his success, but still it was an impressive first outing with a fly rod for anyone.

Kenny's experience at Caddo, and a chenille-bodied, rubber-legged panfish fly called a Bream Killer, has proven an effective combination. There is something about the Bream Killer's slow fall combined with its live rubber legs that makes Caddo bass respond. Despite perfect circumstances for poppers, they don't seem to catch bass like flies that fall slowly.

Kenny recommends dark-colored flies in early spring, when bass are feeding largely on crawfish. Spin-and-bait casters do well with plastic lizards in black and blue, and green and blue, during this period, so flies in those colors are good bets. Chartreuse-and-white flies become effective when the water temperature exceeds 60 degrees. Bass tend to hug cypress roots in water that is six feet deep or less in spring, and respond to slow-falling flies presented close to the cypress.

Caddo's vast shallow-water areas warm quickly in spring, and depending on air temperature and the amount of sun, bass spawning can commence as early as mid February. By spring, these bass are in the post-spawn stage and have moved to deeper water. Fish that live in deeper water may still be spawning in May.

During the bass spawn, chain pickerel stake out bass nests, ready to move in on fry when the opportunity develops. Old Folks Playground, Turtle Shell, Britt's Gap and Hogwallow are good areas to target pickerel during the spawn. A 2 1/2-pound pickerel is a good fish for Caddo, but they can reach four pounds or more there.

Topwater flies become effective around June. Otherwise, flies that resemble sunfish work well in the coves and shallows, streamers are good in channels where shad congregate, and the Bream Killer still catches fish. Kenny says that while Caddo's largest bass will normally be in the lake's mid section, there are more of them in the upper end, and there are shallow areas where bass do survive and can be caught in summer, despite the generally depleted oxygen levels. Possibly a significant rain or cool front can make some shallows temporarily livable, or they move in by day and out to deeper water at night. Much of this shallow water is choked with vegetation throughout summer, and inacces-

sible, but according to Kenny, it is not necessarily devoid of fish.

In the heat of summer, (Kenny says that at Caddo that means it is so hot and humid that you can barely breathe), chain pickerel remain active in shallow weedy water. Streamer flies in blue and white, and chartreuse and white are effective for them as well as bass. Another summer option is rock bass, or goggle eye, as they are often called, which move into the shallows to spawn in summer. Kenny uses a Bream Killer with a split shot for them, because they are reluctant to rise for a fly. He says that if you find a concentration of them you can catch can catch 40 or 50 in a short time; some of which will be big enough to fillet.

Kenny considers areas of mixed vegetation to be the best bass cover at Caddo. Places where hydrilla, milfoil, water hyacinths, and lily pads grow together seem to produce the best fishing. He believes that the vegetation mix produces oxygen at different times and amounts, stabilizing the oxygen level, and fish like that, as well as the shade. On a shallow lake like Caddo, deep spots are not widely available, and shade is vital.

Beginning in late July or August, bass begin schooling in open areas of the lake, wide parts of the channels, and bends where shad are plentiful. A chartreuse, yellow, or blue and white Clouser, or silver Pencil Popper cast to blowups (shad attempting to escape bass) rarely fails.

As summer wanes and the nights cool, the water temperature in Caddo's shallows drops fast, and bass get the urge to gorge before winter. Lilly pad leaves die leaving only the stems for baitfish to hide in, which makes them more vulnerable to bass. Weedless baitfish flies in blue and silver, or chartreuse, worked slowly through the pad stems are effective this time of year, as are poppers. Bass are likely to bury themselves when hooked in the pads, so a strong leader tippet is required. Once winter sets in, bass and sunfish become sluggish, and crappie is about the only game in town, but fly rods and lead-eyed Clousers, streamers with a split shot, or jigs are a good crappie outfit.

There are no fly shops on Caddo Lake, so bring along what you are going to need. If you forget something, the closest one is a Bass Pro Shop in Bosier City, Louisiana, which is not terribly far.

Caddo is a lake of mysteries, and they cannot be solved in a few days. Patterns are difficult to determine, changeable or nonexistent. Cold fronts and wind changes can put the fish down suddenly and for days. It is not like lakes in other areas, and if you are not used to fishing bogeys and bayous it can be tough. Kenny says that if you have only one or two days in your life to fish Caddo, you should hire a guide, or come for the scenery.

⭐ 2

Lake Fork

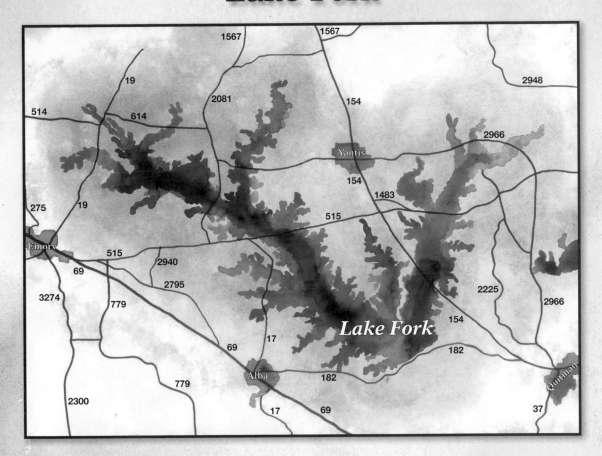

Called "Fork," by locals, Lake Fork is a reservoir on Lake Fork Creek, a major tributary of the Sabine River. It also looks like a fork with two arms, one Lake Fork Creek and the other Caney Creek that produce mirror-image prongs. The 27,689 acre reservoir has a maximum depth of 70 feet, and holds channel catfish, black and white crappie, big sunfish, and white and yellow bass, but it's huge largemouth bass that draw fishermen from all over the world.

The current lake and state record is 18 pounds, but a 19-pounder was found dead, (choked by a big bluegill it had attempted to swallow) and that fish would have almost certainly been Texas' first 20-pounder when it was alive.

One look at this reservoir and it is apparent that there is far more inviting cover to fish than there is time to fish. The Sabine River Authority (SRA), which controls the reservoir, had originally planned to clear most of the timber before filling the lake, but Steve Smith, the project's biologist at the time, convinced the SRA to leave most of it and cut boat lanes

through the stickups, which saved SRA a sizeable chunk of money and a great deal of woody habitat for the bass.

In addition to timber structure, Lake Fork has abundant vegetation. The lake's level varies only a moderate two to four feet, which permits lush weed growth along the shoreline and on the bottom where the depth is 12 feet or less. There is American lotus (lily pads), hydrilla, Eurasina milfoil, coontail, water primrose, water hyacinth, and pennywort, with some cattails in the backs of the coves and creek inlets. Hydrilla, Eurasian milfoil, and water hyacinth are exotics, most likely transferred from ponds upstream, where it was planted as a novelty. Eurasian milfoil is not a problem, but water hyacinth is. The aggressive plant with pretty purple flowers becomes so dense that it cuts off light to other plants and chokes waterways. It must be periodically treated with defoliant.

Hydrilla, often transferred on boat trailers, is capable of growing at depths of fifteen feet in clear water. It can grow from the bottom to the surface in a solid mat.

Rob Woodruff fishing lily pads at Fork.

Hydrilla is a nuisance in some lakes, but at Fork it produces excellent bass habitat. Targeting the hydrilla holes, and its edges, is routine procedure for bass and sunfish.

Fork has historically accounted for all the biggest, and 60-75 percent of the 50 biggest bass ever caught in Texas. Florida-strain largemouth were first put in existing stock ponds that were to be inundated with waterin 1978.

Fork is where the famous Ethel was caught in November 1986 by Mark Stevenson of Plano. Ethel weighed 17 pounds on that day and was the Texas state record. Stevenson kept the huge bass alive in an aerated minnow tank and turned her over to the Texas Parks and Wildlife Department where she became the first entry in the Operation ShareLunker program.

Ethel went to Bass Pro Shops' flagship Outdoor World store in Springfield, Missouri in May of 1987 where she spent the remainder of her life in a 64,000-gallon aquarium. Ethel was the star of the store's aquarium and the daily feeding shows. She was an enormously popular attraction. It is estimated that 20 million customers saw her gently accept goldfish from the divers' hands at the shows.

Ethel had shown no signs of poor heath when she died suddenly on August 5, 1994. She was 28 inches long, with a girth of 32 inches, and conservatively estimated at 20 pounds, making her the largest bass in captivity. She had lived for 19 years—twice the life expectancy of a wild bass. There was an obituary in the Springfield newspaper, and a ceremony for Ethel that included speeches from Mark Stevenson and Bass Pro Shops founder, Johnny Morris.

Bass get almost all the attention from fishermen at Fork, but there is an excellent, and relatively overlooked, sunfish fishery. Bluegill and redear are the dominant sunfish at Fork and both species can weigh over a pound. Yellow bass are native and white bass have been added recently by unauthorized stockings. A monster hybrid yellow/white bass weighing slightly over four pounds was caught in 2003, but white bass are still a relatively infrequent catch. Crappie fishing is also good, and also somewhat overlooked at Fork.

Threadfin and gizzard shad are the primary food fish for bass in Fork. Sunfish are an important secondary forage, as are small yellow bass, catfish, crawfish, frogs, and insects.

Bass between 16-inches, which at Fork is about 2 1/4-pounds, and 24 inches which average 8.9 pounds, must be released, and only one fish longer than 24 inches can be kept per day. Most big bass are caught between February and the end of April, and Fork is a busy place in spring. There are plenty of motels and restaurants in the area, but if you intend to be at Fork when the big bass are being caught it would be wise to make lodging reservations in advance. Don't expect to buy fly-fishing supplies at Fork, the closest fly shops are about 40 miles away in Tyler.

The bass spawning cycle usually starts about mid-February, depending upon the weather and moon. A few warm days in a row and a full moon will cause bass to begin moving out of the deep water and into creek arms. The key to success in early spring is to find the warmest water which, in morning, will be west-facing banks with a south east exposure. In afternoon, east-facing banks with a southwest exposure will have the warmest water. If the water is slightly stained along such banks it will be even warmer because it absorbs more solar radiation than clear water. Once into their pre-spawn cycle, bass tend to stay in one area and move up and down in depth based on water temperature and barometric pressure. On warm, sunny days they will be in the shallows, but move out and down to 10 feet or so at night.

Robert Woodruff, the only full-time fly-fishing guide at Fork, says that fly-fishing will not get good until the water reaches 53 degrees, and things won't really start happening till it hits 60. However, bass will not be so shallow or active in 60-degree water if it was 65 degrees the day before, and consequently 55-degree water will fish well if the water was 50 the day before. Under these conditions, Robert recommends a sink-tip line, with three feet of 16-pound monofilament as a leader, and a slow retrieve in 10 to 12 feet of water, then as the day progresses and the water warms, fishing shallower. If it is necessary to fish on or near the bottom, Rob goes down to a 10- to 12-pound leader, because the fly is more likely to get hung, and 16-pound monofilament is difficult to break and trying is likely to damage line-leader connections.

In early spring Rob recommends big bulky dark flies such as Bunny Leeches, Deceivers, and Rabbit Strip Deceivers. They should be weighted, but not so heavy that they fall like a stone. He prefers them to be pulled down by the sink-tip.

As spring progresses, Rob suggests concentrating on the creeks and watcheing for bedding activity. Several one- to two pound male bass in an area is a good indicator that there are big females nearby in the deeper water, where you cannot see the bottom. Flies that imitate sunfish and water dogs (tiger salamander larva) are effective at this point for females that are still feeding. A big meal that doesn't require much effort looks good to them, and sunfish patterns in olive with an orange bottom also emulate intruders and stimulate their territorial instincts. The colder the water, the slower you should work them.

Unless a cold front moves the fish deeper, a floating line with a seven- to eight-foot leader is appropriate at this point. You are generally going to be fishing six feet of water or less, and even in eight feet of water the fish aren't likely to only be down more than four feet. This is the time to be looking for weed beds, and along weed lines for big bass. A fly called a Sili Shad—designed by Rob to dart about randomly when twitched, like some plastic bass lures do—and neutral buoyancy streamers are good choices at this time when bass are defending territory. Anything that hovers near a nest too long is likely to be attacked, especially sunfish and small bass, even turtles which are abundant at Fork, may be assaulted. In this phase of the spawn, sizable bass will also patrol small areas, swimming in an elliptical circuit, and are prone to attacking anything they perceive as an intruder.

Kevin Storey, Lake Fork's biologist, says there is no evidence that fishing for bass on spawning beds has been detrimental to the bass population. Rob says that if you are going to fish over bedded bass,

use sharp hooks and at least an eight-weight rod to bring the bass in quickly. Don't take the fish out of the water unless you want a picture. For pictures, avoid holding them in the wind, don't lay them on, or let them touch, the boat carpet, and don't touch them with dry hands. Rob's system is to hold the fish in the water while the client gets the camera ready. When he pulls the bass out, the client begins holding his breath. When the client has to take a breath the fish goes back in, if not before.

If there is any other option, and there usually is, Rob will not let clients fish over bedded bass. However, once in a while when conditions are exceedingly tough and it is the only way to get a big bass for a client he will—with discretion. Rob avoids fish on beds in high-traffic areas where other fishermen are likely to come across and catch the bass repeatedly. In his opinion, it's not the first or second time a bedded bass is caught that is the problem, it is the sixth or seventh. A bedded female may get caught, settle down in a half hour and get caught again. Rob has seen freshly caught bass hit flies within minutes of being released, while he was concentrating on another fish nearby.

What Rob will not do is fish for males guarding eggs or fry. You can tell that males are defending eggs or fry if there is no female present, bluegill or other sunfish are lurking nearby, or if you see a cloud of fry in front of the male's face. Under these circumstances, leave the fish alone.

It is common for the bass spawn to be at different stages on the lake. The north part may be in post spawn, the middle in active spawn, and the south part of the lake in pre spawn. This allows fishermen to target actively feeding pre- and post-spawn fish and not bother the bedded bass.

In the post-spawn stage, bass move away from the banks and suspend in the middle of the creeks, or hold around humps in the main lake. They suspend in the middle of the water column and are less active in the initial stages of the post spawn. Depth- or fish-finders are a great help during this period. Groups of bass are likely to be suspended at four or five feet in water that is eight or nine feet deep, and if you can locate them you have a good chance of catching them. A fly presented at their level or slightly above will often draw strikes. They will not move up too far, and will not go down at all for a fly. There is a two-and-one-half to three-foot window for their strike zone. The trick is to find a concentration of bass, determine their depth, and accurately time a sinking or sink-tip line to reach the proper depth. It is a viable, but technical endeavor. Fishing for bass farther north on the lake, that are feeding more aggressively after having gone through this early post-spawn stage, is often an option.

The bass spawn coincides with spring storm season, which is frequently dramatic in this area. Rob

Bass that took popper in spring.

warns fishermen to avoid getting back into coves where they cannot see the sky, and from which you cannot move out quickly. Standing timber, slightly below the surface is so thick that there are vast areas of the lake where you cannot go fast. If a storm surprises you back in a creek there is no way to outrun it.

When the water temperature is at least 60 degrees, and bass are in both pre- and post spawn mode, topwaters become effective. In March and April, you cannot work a topwater too slowly. Some bass may hit a popper that is being worked fast and also a slowly worked one, but it does not work the other way. All the bass will take the slow popper, but only some will take the fast popper. In addition, if you let the rings disappear before you begin working the popper and do it slowly you will catch much bigger bass, at Fork and elsewhere.

May through mid-June is topwater time at Fork. Weed lines and weed beds that open out to deeper water on the main lake are prime targets. Bass hit poppers best in early morning and late evening, but on cloudy days they will go for them all day. Rob likes light and visible white, yellow and chartreuse poppers for general fishing. In early morning or late evening's low light he will go to darker colors, such as black or purple in order to present a more definable silhouette to the bass. Some days bigger ones are more effective, and on other days smaller ones are best. There is no rule for popper size, but there is for working them, and that rule is: keep the rod tip on the water. Rob considers that to be the key detail for working poppers, or any flies, at Fork, and he will remind you as many times as it takes. You can make a popper do more with less effort, eliminate slack, and hook fish better if you keep the rod tip at the surface.

In summer there is still a good topwater bite early. Later in the morning, as the topwater action wanes, Rob suggests using a sinking fly on a sink-tip and fishing the deeper water out from the weeds and weedlines at about 10 feet down. By 10 AM, that tactic will also begin to fail and your choices are limited. Bass can be caught throughout the day at Fork in summer by fishing deep structure with a full-sinking line, but this is a technical and tedious exercise that is exacerbated by extreme heat and not that fun.

During summer, Rob's full-day guide trips begin at four in the afternoon. He stays out till about dark, when a lull in the action usually occurs, then completes the trip beginning the next morning at sunrise and ending at 10:30 or 11:00. This comfortable and practical method is infinitely better than suffering through the middle of the day in the Texas sun and working for a few hard-won fish.

When summer wanes, and after the first cooling rains of September, the bass begin to school, and topwaters work along the lily pads and weedlines. Bass start chasing shad in open water and in the bends of the creeks, and it is the season for baitfish imitations. Rob's Simple Shiner, Clousers, and poppers in silver and blue, chartreuse and white, or anything that resembles a baitfish is going to draw some strikes. This time of year it is good to get into the mouth of a creek, or similar area where bass are known to school, and work cover with Dahlberg Divers and frog imitations; look over your shoulder at the main lake for feeding activity. This pattern lasts into November, and perhaps into December until the water temperature drops to the low 50s.

Winter fly-fishing at Fork is often tedious, but it can yield some big bass. After the shortest day of the year has passed, and there are three warm sunny (warm days can happen at any time of year in Texas) days in a row, you can catch bass in ten feet of water or less, on weedbeds, off main lake points, and off secondary points of major creeks. Bass can also be caught 15 to 20 feet deep with sinking line on humps, points, and old road beds after locating them with a depth finder. Good winter fishing at Fork depends on a warm-weather pattern that cannot be timed far in advance. You must be there when the time is right.

Nearby Lake Monticello is a better bet for winter fishing. Three coal-fired power plants on the 2,000-acre lake make for 85-90 degree water during mid-winter, and bass can be caught on topwater flies in January. Bass don't know about cold water in Monticello, and the spawn begins on the first full moon after the shortest day of the year. Impounded in 1972, Monticello was the premier bass lake in Texas before Fork was created and has produced bass over 14 pounds. Unless the weather is perfect, Rob prefers to take clients to Monticello in winter and sometimes in early spring.

Typical of east Texas reservoirs, Fork is home to a few alligators but they are generally shy and not problematic. You will see some snakes, but rarely little ones, the bass eat most of them before they can grow.

3

Brazos River

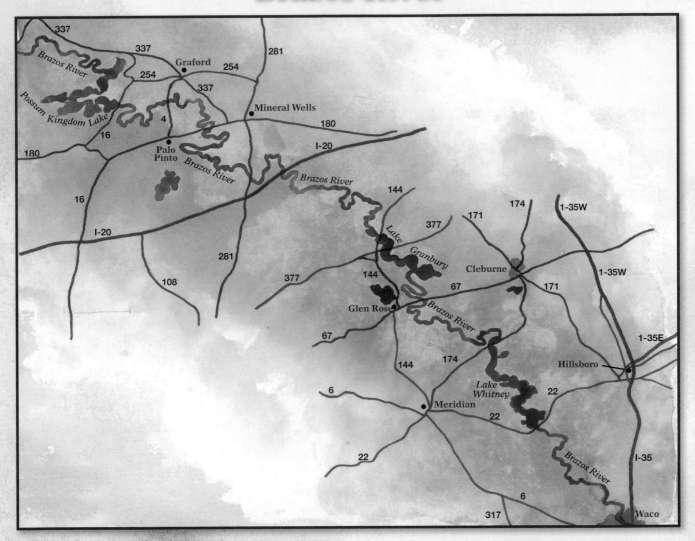

The Brazos River begins in west Texas where the Salt and Double Mountain forks of the Brazos meet in eastern Stonewall County. Both forks flow out of the New Mexico Caprock, an escarpment of hardpan that forms a natural boundary line between the western high plains and the lower rolling plains region of West Texas. The Brazos flows 840 miles from where the forks meet across the state and into the Gulf of Mexico. Each of the forks are about 150 miles long, and they are often added together and the distance applied to the Brazos to make its overall length 1040 miles.

The muddy upper Brazos runs through red dirt and mesquite plains. Both forks carry salt, but the Salt Fork's water can reach 40 parts per thousand, which is a little saltier than open ocean water. The salt comes from natural salt layers and formations left behind by ancient ocean inundations, and from oil-field residue.

The river upstream of the lake is usually turbid and sluggish. A sustained dry spell will allow silt to drop out of the river and clear somewhat, but the upper Brazos is not considered to be good fishing water, although some stripers and white bass run up it from Possum Kingdom Lake. White bass are said to run all the way upriver to the Newcastle area, which would be at least 50 river miles upstream of the lake, and up the Clear Fork, which tends to be a bit clearer than the main Brazos, to the old grist mill at Eliasville.

Most fly-fishing is done in, and downstream of, the main river's three major reservoirs, Possum Kingdom, Granbury, and Whitney where the water is clear. White, striped, hybrid, largemouth, smallmouth, and

Hell's Gate on Possum Kingdom Lake.

spotted bass are the primary target species for fly-fishermen. Secondary species include sunfish, catfish, and rough fish, such as buffalo and carp, that will hit flies in the clear water.

Possum Kingdom, the uppermost Brazos River impoundment, was indeed named for the abundant opossums in the area. PK, as it is called by locals, is a scenic reservoir surrounded by distinctly western topography and tall cliffs. The lower part has extremely clear water, due in part to its salty nature. The clear water makes it a popular scuba-diving destination as well as a good fishing lake. The upper end is not so clear, but normally much clearer than the river.

Located west of Mineral Wells, Possum Kingdom is 15,588 acres with a maximum depth of 145 feet and an average depth of 37 feet. Completed in 1941, it was the Brazos River Authority's first project. PK is a rocky lake that fluctuates considerably in depth, with surface vegetation mostly in the mid to upper reaches, but underwater foliage grows throughout the lake in summer and fall. The lake record largemouth is over 16 pounds, and it has it has produced stripers up to 34-pounds, and smallmouth bass near seven pounds. PK is 75 miles west of Fort Worth, and its proximity to the DFW metroplex and natural beauty makes it a popular lake for pricey water-front homes and big boats.

PK is mostly recovered from a catastrophic golden alga bloom in the winter of 2001. In Texas, golden alga was first confirmed in the Pecos River in 1985, and has since struck lakes in the Canadian, Colorado, and the Brazos river systems. It likes the salt these rivers carry from their west Texas headwaters, and tends to strike in the cooler months when there is less competition from other algae. Golden alga destroys a fish's gills, and during an outbreak makes a golden hue in the water. It can only go down to about 50 feet, and some fish may have survived the bloom by staying below it.

The alga bloom at PK was especially toxic to largemouth and small striped bass, but also thinned the smallmouth numbers considerably. Large stripers and white bass fared better than most fish, in part because many of them had run upstream into the Brazos River and Cedar Creek, where the alga was not a factor.

In the two years following the outbreak, TPWD restocked 1.5 million Florida largemouth, 6.2 million stripers, 435,000 channel catfish, 71,000 blue catfish, and 65,000 smallmouth bass. The fish are growing faster than before the alga outbreak, and PK is fishing well, especially for largemouth. Barring another serious outbreak, it will continue to improve.

TPWD has learned how to combat golden alga with some degree of success, but the one-celled pest is still much of a mystery and everyone remains nervous abut its return. Possum Kingdom's economy took a big hit because of the fish kill. The local Chamber of Commerce estimated a loss of 16 to 18 million dollars for area businesses. Guides disappeared from the lake and guide trips for the remaining few dropped drastically.

The alga's effect on PK's shad population was

threadfin and gizzard shad bounced back quickly, allowing the lake's bass to also make a comeback. Shad are the lake's main bass forage, and Dean Heffner, a Possum Kingdom guide that did not disappear, says that stripers in PK are noticeably fatter than those in Granbury and Whitney reservoirs because of its historically large shad population.

Striped and white bass stay and feed in the open lake most of the year. Watching for shad blow-ups in coves, off points, and in the open lake, then casting silver, white, chartreuse, or yellow streamers or poppers into the mêlée is the primary technique for catching them when they are not in a spawning pattern.

Stripers and white bass begin moving up the channels from the lower lake in fall and by winter they are staging in the upper lake near the river and tributaries. In January and February they move into the river and tributary creeks to spawn. Access is not good on the river and tributaries upstream of the lake, so fishing for them in flowing water generally requires access to private property, but the lower river can be reached by boat from the lake.

Possum Kingdom Lake guide
Dean Heffner with a sand (white) bass.

PK largemouth tend to hold near woody structure, weeds, and docks in the backs of larger coves, and drop-offs—especially those near flats. Smallmouth are most likely to be off primary and secondary points, and where there are rocks and, to a lesser extent, gravel. Largemouths are found throughout the lake, but are most plentiful in the upper portions. Smallmouth inhabit the middle of the lake down to the dam where the water is deep and clear. Dean recommends the mouth of Caddo Creek as a good place to find them.

Black bass at PK consume large numbers of sunfish, but also spend part of their time trapping shad in the backs of coves, on flats, and at the surface like, and sometimes with, stripers and white bass. Dean says that largemouth, spotted, and smallmouth bass will come to the surface for a popper from 30 feet down, sometimes out of the blue—literally. He recommends bone white, yellow and chartreuse poppers that make plenty of noise.

When fishing the coves, Dean looks for muddy water at the back which indicates that feeding fish have roiled the water and may still be feeding. Herons hunting along the banks and turtles out in the water are other indicators of feeding activity. Chartreuse and white or gray and white Clousers with lead eyes work well for bass in these areas. Around the stickups, these flies can be fished like jigs.

Grasshoppers are plentiful at PK. During summer, strong winds blow them into and sometimes across the lake, presenting bass, sunfish and catfish with an easy and substantial surface-feeding opportunity. Typically the wind comes from the south in summer and it works best to fish from the lake's south shoreline, so you can cast with the wind.

Downstream of Possum Kingdom's Morris Sheppard Dam there is a productive stretch of tailwater that runs more than a hundred miles through pretty country, before being backed up by Granbury Lake. Near Possum Kingdom the river flows through rolling rocky hills and low mesas that give it a definite western look. It is not too fast or slow, and there aren't any dangerous rapids. Full generation will make for some heavy and potentially hazardous water, but otherwise it is delightful, easy to wade, and good for fly-fishing.

When not generating, flow from the dam varies by season and conditions. From March first to June 30th the base flow is 100 cubic feet per second (cfs), from the first of July through the end of September, it is 75 cfs, and from October to the end of February it is only 50 cfs. If PK's level drops 6 1/2 feet below the top of the dam, the lake is officially in drought stage, and those flows are cut in half. When the lake goes down 10 feet, flow is completely cutoff and only the 20 cfs leakage from the dam and generators flows into the river. Power generation at PK is of the peaking type, which means generators are turned on to

Brazos River fly-fishing guide Andy Morreau playing white bass in Horseshoe Bend area.

produce power when demand is highest. if the lake is high, 2800 cfs or more can begin flowing from the generators at any time, and the only warning will be the horn at the dam, after which you will have about 15 minutes (don't bet your life on this) to get out. The horn is audible down to the Highway 16 Bridge if the wind and water is quiet and you are paying attention.

During fall, there may be a smell like rotten eggs near the dam. This is hydrogen sulfide, a gas created by organic decomposition in the cold lower layer of lake water, and is typical of Texas reservoirs that are a hundred feet or more deep. When fall weather cools the top layer, it sinks, the middle layer disappears and the top and bottom layers mix, allowing the gas to rise to the surface and flow downstream. The foul-smelling gas evaporates out of the water after flowing over a series of gravel bars, so if you smell this gas at the dam, go downstream. Fish don't like it either and they will do the same.

Largemouth bass are the primary species in this part of the river, but there are also good numbers of striped and spotted bass, sunfish, a few smallmouth, and an occasional walleye. A state-record striper, weighing over 53 pounds, was caught there in the spring of 1999. Stripers are most likely to be in the vicinity of the dam in winter and spring.

Rainbow trout are stocked here in the winter and many fly-fishermen from the Dallas-Fort Worth Metroplex drive out to fish for them. Most trout are stocked at the Highway 16 bridge, but some are also put in downstream at the Highway 4 or Dark Valley Bridge. Relatively few of them move up to the dam, and heavy

water releases at the dam tend to push the hatchery fish, which are unaccustomed to current, downstream.

PK's generator intakes are 60 feet below the lake's surface, and water going through the generators varies from 58 to 61 degrees. With regular generation through summer and early fall, this part of the Brazos could be a year-round trout stream, although hydrogen sulfide could be an issue. As it is, in a relatively cool and rainy year, some trout can survive downriver in pools where depth and spring flow keeps the water temperature tolerable for them. The big hole upstream of Post Oak Bend, more that 20 miles downriver from the dam, produces an occasional trout in summer, as does the pool at the dam.

The huge pool at the base of the dam surely holds many big fish, but a cable with floats is stretched across the river and the upper side is off limits to boats and fishermen. Only a small, shallow section of the pool's tailout is on the downstream side of the cable, and that part is on the far (south) bank. You must scramble down the rocks, wade across the north channel which runs by the access road, and work your way across a big brushy island to the far side where the pool spills into the south channel. That is dangerous. The island, bordered by the two channels, is exactly the wrong kind of place to be caught by a sudden rise. The primary problem would be making it back across one of the channels after the flow increases, but getting caught in the brush would be the worst-case scenario.

I tried fishing the pool and river directly below the dam once, and only once. After fighting my way the flow increases, but getting caught in the brush would be the worst-case scenario.

I tried fishing the pool and river directly below the dam once, and only once. After fighting my way across the island's nearly impenetrable brush to the pool's tailout, I found only shallow water and no fish. It was immediately apparent that getting back to where I had started would be a challenge and if I didn't hear the warning horn, the generators kicked on in less than 15 minutes, or something slowed me down, it would be a race that I could lose.

After nervously fishing the tailout, and the shallow stretch of river a half mile down, to a point near the fish hatchery with no success, I bailed out at the first clearing. There is little holding water between the dam and the big pool upstream of the Highway 16 bridge, and walking it does not seem to be worth the risk. Even after the channels meet, getting out of the stream is inconvenient, due to thick brush and steep banks. The best water between the dam and the Highway 16 bridge is slightly upstream of the bridge so it is more convenient and far safer to wade up from there.

Generation usually means slow fishing, because bass and other warmwater fish stop feeding in the cold water and don't resume until generation stops and the cold water goes downriver. Andy Moreau, a

Highway 16 bridge over Brazos with Morris Sheppard Dam in background.

fly-fishing guide who guides exclusively on the Brazos, says that if there has been generation in the morning the fish will not start biting until about two o'clock. Fishing shallow water out of the current and along weedlines may produce a few fish during generation. The fish he does catch during generation usually come out from behind rocks or other sheltered current and are big. Still, Andy doesn't recommend fishing the PK tailwater during generation. Even 15 miles downstream of the dam, the water can be in the 60s during summer.

Andy likes streamer patterns such as Clousers, Zonkers, and Bead Head Woolly Buggers in size four on this part of the Brazos. Light-colored poppers are effective once the water warms in late April. Hellgrammite patterns are also a good choice, but Andy says that Brazos fish are not particular and he catches them on almost anything when they are in a feeding mood.

There is ample parking at the Highway 16 bridge, where you can launch a canoe or kick boat, or wade far up and down river. The deep hole upstream of the bridge may hold stripers, especially in winter when trout are planted there. Downstream of the bridge is another deep hole, and you can easily walk or wade down to the Flint Bend area. Garland Bend, which is three river miles from the dam is another mile and a half downstream. If the water was running strong when trout were stocked, many of them end up in this area, which is also good for smallmouth bass.

Fortune Bend is seven miles downstream of PK and where Ioni Creek comes into the Brazos. There is a large pool with big rocks that is about 18 feet deep where the creek enters. Andy consistently catches good-sized smallmouth there if the water is not running and cold. You can also get up Ioni Creek about a quarter mile and catch bass until the water gets too shallow to hold fish.

In the lower part of the Fortune Bend area there is a mile-long wadable stretch of "skinny water" that has excellent fishing for smallmouth and largemouth bass and sunfish. When it's fishing good, and it often is, you can spend the whole day there, and if you don't feel like continuing on down the river there are good camping spots. The Brazos flow varies dramatically, so camping at or near the water's edge is inviting disaster.

Downstream of Fortune Bend there is Crawford, Chick and Dalton bends before you come to the Highway 4 crossing which is 19 and a half miles from PK, and a two-day float/fishing trip. This section of the river offers plenty of bass and sunfish, with some drum and plenty of carp. Of particular significance is the second shallow section upstream of Highway 4 which holds big largemouth in addition to the other species.

At the Highway 4 crossing there is a canoe livery, called Rochells, that is a safe place to park your car overnight, this is not the case at the PK dam. It costs to park at Rochells, but according to Andy it's worth it.

From Highway 4 to Granbury Lake there are several private accesses, but public ones are few and getting fewer. You can still get to the river and wade at the Highway 180 Bridge, and at Oaks Crossing a few miles downstream on back roads, which is another place where Andy says you do not want to leave a ve-

The Texas Hill Country

Smallmouth Guadalupe hybrid bass.

DIANE HICKS

Suburban roadrunner.

*Above:
Striped bass.*

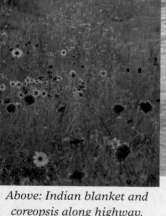

*Above: Indian blanket and
coreopsis along highway.*
*Right: Hill Country
Hospitality—Breakfast at
Raye Carrington's B&B.*

*Above; Float fishing on
San Marcos River.*
*Right:
Upper Guadalupe River*

Bat watchers on Austin's Congress Street Bridge over Town Lake.

The Hill Country is the proverbial "heart of Texas." The state's other regions all border another state, country, or the Gulf of Mexico, but with the exception (on some maps) of a small part that touches the Rio Grande near Del Rio, the Hill Country is completely contained within Texas. This is where you will find Lukenbach, "where Willie, and Walon, and the boys" are supposed to be (Willie does live part time in the Hill Country, but not in Lukenbach).

When you are in the Hill Country there can be no doubt that you are in Texas. The height and configuration of the hills and the sheer limestone bluffs along the rivers are somewhat reminiscent of the Ozarks, but the cypress, mesquite, and live oaks are unmistakably Texas. The hills are part of the Edwards Plateau, the region's most significant natural feature. It and its associated aquifer are the source of the springs that are the source of the beautiful streams. All the prime Hill Country streams are born of and sustained by springs. Rain is far too unreliable. Without the springs, the streams would be dry washes most of the time, and flash floods the rest. However, it is water, not drought that poses the greatest threat to Hill Country streams and the fish that live in them. Minor floods are a common and anticipated occurrence from which the fish

and streams quickly recover. Big floods move rocks, scour out vegetation, and fill in holes with sediment, after which it requires years for the rivers to heal.

The Edwards Plateau rose out of the ocean about 100 million years ago. What is now the coastal plain was then a mountainous highland and northwest Texas was a sea. The land masses mysteriously reversed and the northwest Texas sea became high ground. Limestone, deposited by the ancient sea, eroded when exposed to the elements forming cavities and conduits capable of holding and transferring water. Under the Edwards layer another layer of limestone that is much less permeable served to trap water above. When the area was again inundated, relatively impermeable sediments were deposited above the cavities and conduits sealing them from above. Where the Edwards layer remained exposed became the Edwards Aquifer's recharge zones. Where faults blocked the aquifer's flow, pressure forced the water to the surface in the form of springs, and these springs are what forms the rivers.

The Hill Country was settled (in the European sense, the natives thought it was already settled), in large part, by German immigrants in the mid 1800s, and they imprinted the area's culture. Fredericksburg, Bourne, Gruene, and Kreutzberg are some examples of the many German-named communities. Germans are the largest European-derived ethnic group in Texas, and in 1850 constituted five percent of the state's population. There are bed & breakfasts, shops, and restaurants with German themes throughout the Hill Country.

Austin, the Texas capitol, is a pretty city that straddles the Balcones Fault Line. The west side of town is Hill Country and the east side is blackland prairie. The University of Texas, and its 52,000 students, help enhance a large and obvious counter culture (you will see "Keep Austin Weird," bumper stickers), that is not so apparent in other Texas cities. Leftist Bohemians, high-tech workers and executives, politicians, and conservative Texans all coexist within this city.

Live music is a big part of the entertainment scene and Austin considers itself to be the live music capitol of the world. Most people are aware of "Austin City Limits", and also with many Austin personalities. A list of the big-name stars and acts that got their start, made it big, or are otherwise associated with Austin would be extensive and include, Willie Nelson and the Dixie Chicks. Everyone has played there. There are more than a hundred places in town where you can listen to live music every night.

Austin affords the opportunity to stay in town and mix city entertainment and Hill Country fly-fishing. The Guadalupe, San Marcos, Blanco, and Llano can all be fished on day trips from Austin, and the Colorado runs thought it. Travis, Austin, and Lady Bird lakes are within the city limits.

The Congress Street Bridge over Lady Bird Lake, in the central city, is home to North America's largest urban bat colony. When the bridge was reconstructed in 1980, crevices were created that caused the established bat population to swell exponentially. This bothered some people, but eventually the city came to appreciate the bats. The Mexican free-tailed bats arrive from Mexico in mid-March. In June, the females which comprise most of the colony, give birth to one pup and then they all leave in November. Each evening hundreds of people gather on the bridge and the lawn of the *Austin-American Statesman* newspaper to watch the show, which is most spectacular in July and August. Ooos and aaahhhs, like one hears at fireworks shows, emanate from the crowd as up to one and a half million bats stream out from the bridge for their nightly insect hunt.

On the south side of town is the Lady Bird Johnson Wildflower Center. Founded in 1982 by Mrs. Johnson and actress Helen Hays, it is dedicated to educating people on the value, necessity, and beauty of native plants. The center moved to its present location in 1995 and now has 279 acres, with 15 acres of striking display gardens. The gardens, nature and interpretive trails are maintained by 47 full-time employees, and

about 400 volunteers. The center's tasteful collection of buildings have metal roofs from which rainwater runs off to be collected in cisterns and storage tanks on the grounds for use in the gardens. With normal rainfall, the system supplies 25 to 40 percent of the center's watering requirements, and during a high rainfall years, considerably more. Of course the Wildflower Center's native Texas plants require far less water than the exotics.

Hill Country Rivers and Streams

There are 3700 named streams and 15 major rivers in Texas, but, according to the Texas Parks and Wildlife Department, only 21 percent of them flow year round. It takes a huge watershed, or springs, or both, for a stream to flow throughout the Texas summer. Springs occur all around Texas but they are concentrated in the Texas Hill Country where water from the Edwards Aquifer flows, and in some cases, gushes to the surface. Hill Country streams are a delight to look at, and to fish. They appear to be cypress-lined trout streams, but the choppy riffle water holds Guadalupe bass rather than trout. Native northern largemouth live in the same rivers but are inclined to haunt the slower, deeper water of big pools, so each fish has their niche and they tend not to overlap. Smallmouth and hybrid bass may be situated between the largemouth and Guadalupes. Longear, redbreast (called yellow bellies), redear, and green sunfish, along with warmouth and bluegill inhabit all parts of streams, and Rio Grande perch are found in the pools.

Joey Lin, a Hill Country guide and outfitter, says that with the exception of the clearest of Hill Country streams it is unnecessary and counterproductive to use light tippets and long leaders. Tippet size is more related to fly size than stealth. A six-foot leader with a 1X tippet will serve in most situations, and will not twist the leader when casting big wind-resistant flies. Tippets in 2 or 3X can be useful for small sunfish flies or when you need the fly to sink quickly.

Joey advises anglers not to be overly concerned about fly patterns. Color, size, sink rate, hook configuration, and durability (you can catch dozens of bass and sunfish in a day on these rivers) are the issues he considers. Rubber-legged cork poppers, foam grasshopper patterns with rubber legs, streamers such as Woolly Buggers, Clousers, and Deceivers, and hellgrammite patterns are all good for the Hill Country.

Access makes streams and rivers far less convenient than reservoirs, but in the summer heat, rivers are likely to provide better fishing. Many, if not most, of the fishermen I see along Texas rivers and streams are fly-fishing; reservoirs seem to draw off most other serious fishermen. Texas rivers and streams are considered to be underutilized by TPWD.

Guadalupe River

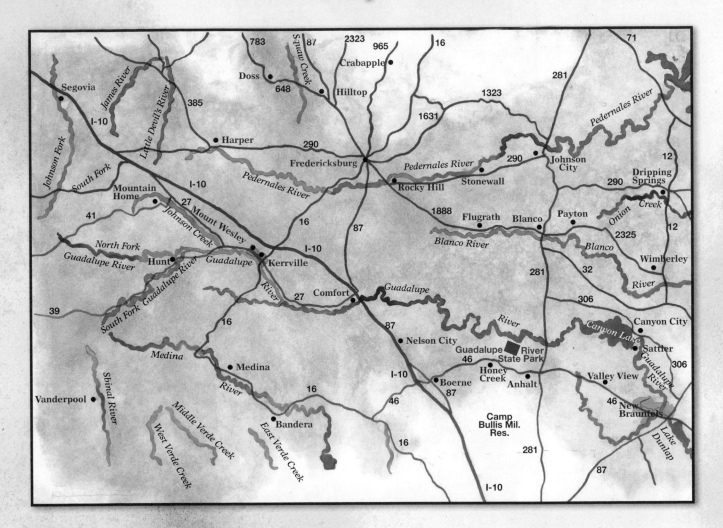

The Guadalupe, sometimes pronounced by Texans as "Gwadaloop," or "Gwad," is Texas' most popular recreational river. Its cool clear water is ideal for swimming, whitewater canoeing and kayaking, floating, tubing, and fishing. At 8,240 acres, Canyon Lake, the Guadalupe's major reservoir, is a popular windsurfing, sailing, and scuba diving destination. The lake has abundant white and striped bass, good populations of largemouth and some smallmouth, plus sunfish, crappie, and catfish.

The main Guadalupe begins where the north and south forks converge near Hunt, in Kerr County. The forks have no distinct starting point, small springs add water incrementally till they begin to run steadily about 20 miles upstream of the junction. The south

fork is known for its summer camps, and the area around Hunt is prized property where wealthy and influential Texans live or spend summers at their "dream ranches." Classic lodges and pleasant bed & breakfasts can be found throughout the area. Average stream flow at the forks has varied between 40 to over 200 cfs from 1966 to 2002. Peak and low flows would range from astronomical to almost nothing—typical of Texas streams. The river also supplies water and power for local residents and nearby municipalities.

Both forks have deep pools and good-sized bass and sunfish, with some access—more on the south fork. The public accesses are well used and the fish are less inclined to be cooperative in their vicinity. Some lodges and other businesses on the forks allow access to fishermen for a fee, and these stretches tend to fish better. The forks are wadable, but deep pools, some of which are formed by dams, are interspersed along the streams and are too deep to wade. Land along the forks is private and going up and around the deep spots is not an option without permission. The forks are best fished by floating, which involves some portaging around dams and low crossings.

From the forks' convergence, the Guadalupe flows 640 miles to the Gulf, where it enters Guadalupe Bay, a sub-bay of San Antonio Bay, southeast of Victoria. The upper portion runs through the Edwards Plateau where it is lined with bald cypress and limestone bluffs. Its character begins to change from Hill Country stream to coastal river as it crosses the Balcones fault line at New Braunfels and Interstate 35. Downstream of this point the limestone bluffs disappear, the river slows, and there are more gravel bars. There are several road crossings where the river can be accessed, and six small hydroelectric power dams and reservoirs that offer accessible fishing.

The river's namesake fish, the Guadalupe bass, northern largemouth, and channel catfish are common in the upper river and present in much of the middle section. According to TPWD records, smallmouth bass were planted from 1974 to 1979 in the river upstream of Canyon Lake. They have done well in the river, too well according to Dr. Gary Garrett, a

Canyon Lake Tailwater

TPWD fisheries scientist, who has provided many of the black bass facts in this book. Smallmouth have seriously endangered the native Guadalupes. TPWD is now stocking Guadalupes in Johnson Creek, a major tributary of the upper river, in hopes of eventually overwhelming the smallmouth genes. It is an expensive project, but that is all there is to be done. If successful in the Guadalupe, the program will probably be tried on other streams. Smallmouths were stocked

Guadalupe River State Park.

in Canyon Lake till 1989 and they are still present in diminished numbers.

Upstream of Comfort, the river is shallow and narrow, with several small dams, and quite scenic. Downstream of Comfort and Waring the river widens and normal flows are sufficient for floating. From Waring to FM 3160 there are several crossings from which you can access the river, including FM 3160, and numerous small rapids. The 22-mile section from FM 3160 to Rebecca Creek is one of the most scenic sections of river in Texas. There are at least 55 rapids in this stretch. Most are no problem, but there are four that can be trouble. Rock Pile Rapids, about one mile downstream of 3160, where large rocks restrict passage is the uppermost. Two miles farther is Dog Leg Rapids where the gradient is particularly steep and the river makes a sharp turn. A mile and one half past FM 311 is Mueller Falls. A chute to the left can be run by experienced whitewater paddlers, but running the main falls is not recommended. Rust Falls, slightly upstream of Rebecca Creek, cannot be run, but it also has a chute that can. All of these obstacles can be portaged. There are also six road crossings in this stretch. Some provide access, some can be floated under, and some can't.

Guadalupe River State Park is in this stretch. It is a pretty place, with facilities, and a long stretch of wadable water that holds a good number of Guadalupes, smallmouth, and hybrids. Despite being only 45 minutes from San Antonio, it seems remote during the off season. The river is already sizable at this point, but can be waded during moderate flows and crossed at the "rapids"—a long stretch of fast, rocky pocket water within the park. Guadalupes hold in the moving water at the foot of the rapids, through the long stretch of choppy fast water, and for some distance downstream. In addition to some chunky Guadalupes, I caught three smallmouth bass that appeared to be pure where the choppy water slows to a long smooth glide. Walking downstream of the rapids takes you to some excellent bass water and eventually out of the park, where you no longer have the legal luxury of walking above the high-water line. There is a sign to that effect at the park boundary.

The river above Canyon Lake is not so fertile as the lower river, and fish do not get so large as they do downstream. Upstream of Canyon, the main forage is minnows of which Texas and blacktail shiners are the most important, but crawfish and aquatic insects are also available. Near the lake, reservoir fish can be caught in the river. There is a boat ramp near Rebecca Creek from which motor boats can be launched, and fishrmen can reach the river without having to cross open water. A mile or two up from the ramp is an another area known as the "rapids," a shoal area where white and some striped bass spawn in the gravel. Florida-strain largemouths and other reservoir fish can also be caught in the first few miles of river upstream of the lake.

Built on the edge of the Hill Country to spare towns along the lower river from floods, Canyon Dam was completed and began to back up the Guadalupe in 1964. The steep sided river canyons can handle flows of 40,000 to 50,000 cfs, but the lower Guadalupe exceeds its banks at 30,000 cfs and in some flat places at 13,000 cfs.

Canyon Lake water is used for irrigation, industry, and municipal water supplies by the Guadalupe Blanco River Authority (GBRA), which has rights to the water in the conservation pool. The top of the conservation pool is 909 feet above sea level, GBRA controls water releases below this level, and the U.S. Army Corps of Engineers controls releases when the lake is higher or in flood pool. Water releases from the dam also power several small downstream hydroelectric operations, and a powerhouse with two generators was added to Canyon Dam in 1989.

The dam has a 10-foot diameter opening at its base from which water flows constantly into the river. Canyon is 125 feet deep so this water is easily cold enough to support trout. The GBRA power plant located slightly down from the opening is "run of the river" and during normal flows, water is diverted through it. The two generators operate between 90 and 580 cfs and can produce 5670 kilowatts. There is a bypass valve that allows a maximum of 1100 cfs to pass through the powerhouse. Flows more than 1100 cfs are considered "flood" releases, and must be passed through the conduit directly into the tailwater. The flow cannot be split between the river and the powerhouse, and the generators do not kick on and raise the water level dangerously as do peak demand type tailwaters.

The Guadalupe Tailwater was first stocked with rainbow trout in 1965 by the Lone Star Brewing Company of San Antonio. Before stocking the tailwater, Lone Star was buying trout from Missouri and putting them in tanks at boat shows in Houston, San Antonio, and Dallas for kids to catch. Harry Jersit, Lone Star's president at the time, was also one of the Texas Game and Fish Commission (now Texas Parks and Wildlife Department) directors. Harry thought it would be beneficial to the Commission, and good public relations for the brewery, to stock the Canyon tailwater with trout. After the Commission checked the water temperature and found it cold enough for trout, Lone Star ordered trout for the tailwater. These trout were not left over from a trout pond. Leftover trout were given away after the boat shows, and the boat shows to which Lone Star supplied trout were only in San

Antonio, Houston, and Dallas, not at Canyon Lake where it would be more or less convenient to haul them to the dam.

According to Jerry Retzloff, now retired from Lone Star, this was the first time trout had been stocked in Texas. The trout were put in with great fanfare that included search lights and amplified music. The favorite baits were gum and cheese—probably Velveeta. Catches were monitored and recorded.

Lone Star, now owned by Pabst Brewing Company, continued to stock the tailwater on an annual basis until Texas Parks and Wildlife took over, and the Guadalupe River Chapter of Trout Unlimited (GRTU) was formed. Since then it has developed into a year-round trout river, but not without a great deal of work, conflict, and expense.

After Canyon Dam was constructed, the Guadalupe was a coldwater stream nine or ten months a year and a warmwater stream the rest. The native warmwater species could not endure this scenario, so without trout there would be no significant fishery in the tailwater, and without increased summertime flow there would be no trout throughout the year. August was the most critical month and when Canyon Lake dropped to a certain level GBRA reduced the flow to a trickle. During construction of the hydro-electric plant there were some no-flow periods. Otherwise, the releases typically varied between 50 and 3000 cfs. This was no way to run a trout stream.

Trout fishing on the Guadalupe is and always has been popular, and many Texans considered having a real trout stream in their state a cause worthy of a fight. There was already a Guadalupe Chapter of Trout Unlimited (GRTU), which was, and is, the only chapter in Texas, and the largest in the nation with a membership of about 4,000. Something had to be done to secure sustaining coldwater releases during summer, and the Guadalupe Chapter, with the support of the national organization, set about to do it.

There is no hydropower pool at Canyon Lake and water cannot be held for power, only consumptive use. GBRA applied for new water rights that would allow them to hold more water, by subordinating the senior hydropower rights downstream to the junior rights of consumptive users. Essentially, GBRA would be able to store and sell more water, and release less into the river, an arrangement that held ominous potential for people who lived on the lake and river, and the trout fishery. GRTU commenced raising funds for legal maneuvering. As a post on the chapter's message board put it, "send lawyers, guns, and money."

There was never a lawsuit and none threatened. GRTU was not a water-rights holder and therefore not entitled, under Texas waterrights law, to sue. Instead, GRTU was able to file for intervener status with the

Diane Hicks fishing the deep hole upstream of "The Island," in the Guadalupe's trophy trout section.

Federal Energy Regulatory Commission because of GBRA's power plant at Canyon Dam. The chapter was granted status to contest GBRA's plan and had two hearings in front of the Texas Natural Resources Council where GBRA argued against their status. GRTU prevailed, and GBRA determined that it was in their best interest to come to a settlement, and GRTU was agreeable. The chapter had already raised nearly $90,000 to get to this point, but it would have taken half a million for a protracted challenge. It was a win-win situation. GRTU got what it wanted and GBRA could go about its business acquiring water rights. Water was guaranteed for the river, and none was, or ever will be, diverted from human consumption. Still, some were unhappy, or perhaps misunderstood the deal. A Comal County judge said, "They are putting the life of a fish that is not even native to that river above the health, welfare and well-being of people in a seven county area."

The agreement, effective July 17, 2001, stated that GRBA would remit $75,000 to GRTU for its legal expenses, and would release water sufficient to sustain trout for ten to 13 miles downstream of the dam through the summer months. GBRA agreed to minimum daily releases (averaged over 24 hours) from Canyon Reservoir during May, June, July, August and September, provided that Canyon Lake's reached a level greater than 909 feet at some point between January 1 and September 30 of that year. If the level was reached before May, water releases were guaranteed throughout the summer, otherwise the required releases did not start until the level was reached—if and when that was. Provided that the 909 "trigger" was reached before May, GBRA promised to release a minimum of 140 cfs from May 1 to May 15, 170 cfs from May 16 to May 31, 210 cfs from June to June 14, 240 cfs from June 15 to June 30, and 200 cfs from then through the end of September. In a severe drought, the trigger would not be met and GBRA would not have to uphold the agreement. In a worst-case scenario, the trout stream could shrink from 10 to about two miles of river. However, GBRA has the right to sell water, and if that water is sold downstream in summer when demand is highest, the results would not be so bad. Whatever the case, Guadalupe trout are better off than they were before the agreement, and GBRA and GRTU now have a good relationship.

Following a drought that began in early 2005, Canyon Lake's level was 905.46 on April 30th 2006 and the trigger was not met. Drought continued through the summer and the lake never rose to 909. Biologist Steve Magnelia says that the lake's outflow was matched to its inflow, (40 to 50 cfs) through much of the summer; roughly a quarter of what the flow would have been if the trigger had been met. The first three miles downstream of Canyon Dam remained cold, but downstream water temperatures reached 80 degrees. Steve did not receive reports of dead trout, but believes it was inevitable that many did die. There was no evidence of them moving upstream to cooler water, but some may have survived in the deepest parts of the deepest pools.

Fly-fishing guide Bill Higdon fighting a trout in the pool downstream of Devil's Playground.

TPWD stopped stocking the Guadalupe once it became apparent that the trigger would not be met, and trout population dwindled significantly, but by late September, the Guadalupe had cooled to the point that TPWD, and TU could resume their stocking schedules Ironically, the Guadalupe trout fishery's greatest threat is too much water, now that the minimal release problem has been addressed. The Guadalupe, like every other Texas river, is prone to flooding, and big destructive hundred-year ones seem to come far more often than every hundred years. There was a flood in 1998 that wrecked the trout fishery. Then, in the summer of 2002 a vicious low-pressure area sat on the Guadalupe's watershed and dumped about 40 inches (almost an average year's rainfall) in less than a week. The Spring Branch gauge on the river upstream of Canyon Lake showed a peak flow of 107,000 cfs on July 3rd, and a depth of 43 feet where two is average. Canyon Lake's level reached an all-time high of 950.32 on July 6th. That is more than seven feet above the spillway crest and 41 feet above the conservation pool level. It was obvious that this 400-year flood was going to send a great deal of water down the Canyon Dam's spillway channel, through which lake water had never run and no one knew exactly what would happen.

A flow estimated to be in excess of 60,000 cfs poured down the spillway channel at the flood's peak. Fortunately, the flood was caused by steady rain and the water rose gradually, the spillway did its job, the dam was not over topped, and a projected 125,000 cfs flow downstream at New Braunfels was averted. Unfortunately, many people lost homes, businesses, and jobs, but no one died. Water temperatures went well into the 80s and all, or nearly all (some say a few survived),

the trout were gone, and a herd of trout-eating stripers came down the spillway and settled in the tailwater, then proceeded to wreak havoc on the new trout.

In 2004 sustained wet weather in spring and early summer filled Canyon Lake and the Corps of Engineers was forced to release massive amounts of water on a continual basis. As the weather continued to warm, the lake's surface water also warmed. Water releases from Canyon come only from the bottom of the lake where the cold pool, or hypolimnion, that Guadalupe trout depend upon for survival lies. The hypolimnion was depleted and warm surface water replaced it. Instead of releasing the normal 200 cfs of 60-degree water, Canyon Dam was releasing flows up to 5500 cfs of 77-degree water. Once again, the trout were lost and it wasn't until the following winter that the water had cooled and the flow had subsided to the point that the Guadalupe could be restocked. If such disasters could be avoided trout would live, grow, and reproduce in the Guadalupe as they have proved they can.

Public access to the trout-stream section is limited and somewhat complicated. You can get to the river immediately downstream of Canyon Dam on either side for free. On the south side it is possible to walk and wade downriver about a mile before deep water prevents you from continuing. There is some good riffle water, deep pools, and deep channels in the limestone bedrock running parallel with the current in this section. There is no put-in in this section, except at the dam which would require a long portage from the parking lot down to the river, so this part of the river is rarely floated.

Campgrounds, outfitters, and other businesses on the river will grant access and allow parking for a fee—usually three to five dollars. Once in the river you can continue until deep water and private property keeps you from going up and around. TPWD has leased access at the Cliffs, which are located at the third crossing (you will hear much about the "crossings," which are crossings of the Guadalupe on River Road, starting with the first in New Braunfels and working upstream to the fourth in the trophy water). This access offers no bank fishing, only wading, and fishermen are advised not to wade if the flow exceeds 500 cfs. There is another TPWD access slightly downstream of the first River Road crossing at Camp Huaco (pronounced like Waco) Springs where you must park your car in a designated area and walk to the river to avoid a daily access fee. There is a mile of bank access and good wading at this spot. Both accesses are free till March 17, and trout are stocked at both locations. TPWD's accesses change periodically, so there is no guarantee they will remain the same from year to year.

special conditions apply. Fees for participation in the lease program vary, but the cost is approximately $95, $45 for a spouse, and $10 per guest pass with a limit of six; children 10 to 17 are free. The lease program is open only to Trout Unlimited members.

The 12-mile trout section of the Guadalupe is not difficult to wade provided you have felt soles. Some of the limestone bedrock is slick, and there are rocky irregular sections of fast water that require careful maneuvering, but with a flow of 200 and 300 cfs you can wade fish much of the river and cross in places. Flows in excess of 300 cfs make the river deep and swift, and wading should be left to those with swift-water wading experience. At 500 cfs or more, the river is unwadable and should be fished from a boat.

Bill Higdon, who lives and guides on the Guadalupe, likes 300 to 500 cfs for floating, because many hazards are covered. Lower flows mean more obstacles, and higher ones require a level of whitewater skill to negotiate the class II and III rapids. Bill uses a Clackacraft drift (or McKenzie River) boat that only drafts three to four inches with two fishermen—three inches less than a similarly loaded canoe. His boat is delightfully comfortable and stable to float in and fish from. Bill can safely float the river up to 2000 cfs, and catch fish in sheltered water.

Ponderosa Bridge with scrape where floating house hit it during flood.

At the 300 to 500 cfs the river is not beyond the limits of a novice canoeist, but because this is a rocky tailwater in which flows and obstructions can change, Bill recommends intermediate canoeing skills. There are countless rocks, four concrete weirs,

GRTU also leases access in various places along the river where members who have paid the fees can fish and where the club stocks larger trout than what the state puts in, along with some brown trout. Conditions for these leases vary, and some limit the number of anglers that can use them. On one lease only two fishermen can be on the property at a time, so anglers put up a flag to notify others that the lease is being used. Some leases are annual and unlimited, others require certain parking restrictions, and others are good only till March 31st. Leases and their restrictions can change, so first-time lease participants are required to attend TU's lease orientation classes where they learn where the leases are and what

and two particularly tricky rapids in the trout water part of the river. The two- to three-foot-tall weirs were built long ago to deepen the water behind them for irrigation pumping. They are not a serious navigation hazard within the 300-500 cfs range. You can pop over the first one which is upstream of the trophy water and the shortest. The second is about a quarter mile downstream of where the trophy water begins, and it poses no problem as long as you don't go over sideways. The third, about a hundred yards down from the second weir and upstream of a long choppy run called Kanz Run, has a six-foot section missing that clean-up crews knocked down with heavy equipment, after the flood of 1998, through which a boat or raft can pass. The last weir in the trout water is between the second and third crossing. This one cannot be run safely, but there is a chute on the left that can. Although these weirs are not considered to be dangerous at regular flows, if you have not been down the river before it would be wise to get out and look before you run them. Low flows create more of an obstacle course of protruding rocks and shallow water below weirs that can cause a boat to capsize.

Of greater concern are Devils Playground and Bad Rock rapids. Devils Playground, reportedly named so because of all the canoes that turn over there, is a long, curving stretch of rough boulder-strewn white water. With less than 300 cfs there are protruding boulders that can, and will, capsize a canoe. Another quarter mile down the river is Bad Rock Rapids, justly named for one big rock in the middle of the current V that is a challenge to avoid because the current takes you right at it. Smacking into Bad Rock would be a jarring experience, quite possibly followed by a capsize. It can be dodged by sticking to the left side. In low flows this is problematic because there is precious little water on the left side in which to float. It is however, easy to walk a canoe past the rock. Each of these problem areas offer excellent riffle and pocket water for nymph fishing.

Pale morning duns, blue wing olives, and Tricos hatch on sunny days throughout the season, which is considered to be from mid-October through May when the water is coldest and tubes are not present. PMDs ranging from size 16-20 hatch from around 10 AM to 3 PM, BYOs in the size 18 range start early and finish mid to late morning. Tricos are usually on the water from late morning to sunset. A size 14-16 slate wing drake hatch occurs in the lower section of the river, usually downstream of the third crossing. Prolific midge hatches occur all year in riffles, but peak on sunny days from December through February. In early summer, there are *Hexagenia* hatches at night, they are size 10-12.

Streamer flies, Woolly Buggers in particular, are always good on the Guadalupe. Olive Bead Heads with Flashabou in the tail are standard, but the rubbe-legged version is also a good choice. Guadalupe brown trout tend to hold in deep water and they are frequently caught on streamers using a sink-tip line. The Guadalupe's current is strong, and getting the fly down is essential for maximum success for browns and rainbows.

Nymphs are the most reliable flies for the Guadalupe. High-sticking in the fast water always works, but in the pools and deeper runs Bill recommends using a two-fly rig—attractor and point fly. He likes a San Juan Worm or big Hare's Ear on top, and a size 18-20 point fly, such as a Hare's Ear or RS2 emerger pattern.

Midge nymphs with a flash wing, Prince Nymphs, and egg patterns are also recommended. The peach/orange egg pattern attractor with a natural San Juan Worm point fly works well on the Guadalupe, as it seems to everywhere.

Though Guadalupe fish are stocker trout, they quickly learn to be cautious and selective. Bill says that a 5X tippet is as heavy as you want for nymph fishing, but you may be able to use 4X or 3X with streamers in deep water. The clearer the water the smaller the fly, and the lighter and longer the leader needs to be.

The uppermost section, from the dam to the easternmost crossing of Highway 306, has no special regulations. You may keep five trout of any size or species. This is the coldest water and best habitat in the river, and the state stocks this stretch several times a year with 10- to 13-inch trout. The next 12 miles downstream of this point to the second crossing is designated trophy water and one trout, of any species, 18 inches or longer per day is the limit. On the Trout Unlimited leases, catch and release is mandatory. GRTU stocks the trophy section with approximately 10,000 trout per year up to 22 inches. These trout and the ones stocked by the state, come from Crystal Lake Fisheries on the headwaters of Hunter Creek, near Ava, Missouri. GRTU also stocks brown trout on a limited basis—typically 1000 or so 1 1/2- to two-pound browns a year. Brown trout come from Crystal Springs Trout Farm in Cassville, Missouri, which is associated with Crystal Lake.

The second crossing on River Road is the official end of the trout water and special regulations. TPWD uses that point because it is the farthest downstream area that trout could possibly survive in summer. The trout water to bass water transition zone normally begins miles upstream, but between the second and first crossings the transition is complete. Trout are sometimes caught downstream of the second crossing, and the regulations are same as in the upper three miles.

Winter is prime time for trout fishing on the Guadalupe. Although the river is cold enough to sustain trout through summer, higher than ideal water temperatures stress them. Also, hordes of tubers descend upon the Guadalupe in late spring and don't thin out till the weather cools in fall. Except for occasional mid-week trips, Bill deserts the Guadalupe and concentrates on other rivers from Memorial Day through Labor Day.

Downstream of the trout water, the river loses its chill but retains its fast water character all the way to New Braunfels and I 35. This stretch is considered to be Texas' most consistent white water and is immensely popular with thrill-seeking canoeists and kayakers, and during warm weather, tubers. There are several rapids, that require skill to run, especially when flows are high.

Guadalupe rainbow.

Slightly upstream, and surrounded by New Braunfels, is the quintessential tourist town of Gruene (pronounced "green"). There is a cluster of interesting shops, restaurants, galleries, a classic dance hall that is considered to be Texas' oldest, a fly shop, and several quaint bed and breakfasts, including the Gruene Mansion Inn. This large B&B sits on a bluff above the Guadalupe, and has a variety of lodging choices including a string of rooms overlooking a deep-green pool downstream of the Class III Gruene Rapids.

In New Braunfels, Comal Spring, the largest spring in Texas, adds an average of 300 cfs via the 2 1/2- mile (billed as the nation's shortest river) Comal River. The river is completely contained within the town, but has some interesting opportunities for fly-fishermen. Marcus Rodriguez, half of the Hill Country guide service, Guides of Texas, fishes it for pleasure. He recommends 14-acre Landa Park Lake, a crystal-clear weedy lake on the Comal that holds an astonishing number of fish. Wading in and floating on the lake is prohibited, but there is plenty of shoreline to walk. Marcus warns fly-fishermen to watch out for people walking on the path behind, and also the park train which runs close to the water. The lake gets a great deal of pressure, but the fish respond well to flies and become active at some point every day. He doesn't do much blind casting, but waits for a bass to go after something then casts to the disturbance. Comal bass have Florida genes and are extremely dark with a golden sheen.

You can put a kickboat or canoe in the Comal, downstream at Hinman Island, and go up or downstream, but be cautious. There is a small dam and a couple of chutes in this stretch that borders the Schlitterbahn, which is the world's most popular water park. The area will be crowded in summer, and people will be in the chutes. If you run a chute without looking, you are likely to hit someone.

There is a takeout point on the Comal about one hundred yards before it meets the Guadalupe, and more on the Guadalupe that are not far. The Comal is a busy place and fishes best either in the off season or extremely early.

Not far downstream, the San Marcos enters with an average 400 cfs that is roughly half from San Marcos Springs and half from the Blanco River. In a short stretch, the river gets much bigger, then gradually loses its clarity as it flows through farm country on its way to the coast, as Hill Country rivers do when they drop off the Edwards Plateau. There is a series of small impoundments and a good deal of fishable river on the east side of Interstate 35.

5

Llano River

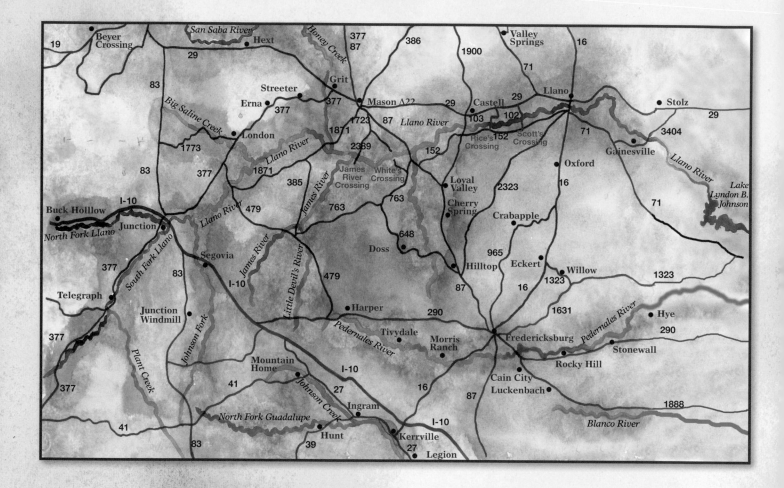

Llano means plain in Spanish, but the country through which the Llano River flows does not fit the name. There are deep canyons with tall limestone and sandstone bluffs and a rocky beauty throughout the river's course. Unlike some Hill Country rivers, such as the Blanco and Guadalupe, the Llano's banks are not shaded by cypress or pecan trees. It is wide open and close to shadeless, with an irregular brushy shoreline that rarely interferes with a back cast.

The Llano begins in the central Kimble County town of Junction where its two spring-fed forks meet. The north fork flows intermittently along Interstate 10 toward eastern Kimble County from its start in central Sutton County. The south fork rises along Texas

377 in northern Edwards County and closely follows the highway to Junction. The Llano proper then continues about 100 miles to the upper reaches of Lake Lyndon B. Johnson, (always referred to as LBJ) on the Colorado River near Kingsland.

The Llano's north fork averages about 40 cfs in Kimble County with some fishable water but without a fresh rain it will not float well. Access is restricted, and fishing or floating the north fork without permission of private landowners will be problematic.

Llano is formed by several small springs and seeps west of Roosevelt in Sutton County. Two larger springs, Adams and Logan, provide the majority of its water. The north fork is characterized by shallows, still pools, and small rapids. Its low and sometimes intermittent flow is not ideal for Guadalupe bass, but there are some deep, vegetated pools that hold big largemouth. Historically, there were more and larger springs and pools of live water along the north fork, before the water table was lowered by wells.

The Llano's south fork has nearly twice the north fork's flow and is fishable all the time and floatable most of the time. The south fork rises at Llano Springs and continues north along Highway 377 where several small springs enter. More substantial springs, Tanner, 700, and Big Paint swell the river south of Telegraph, bringing its flow up to a minimum of 65 cfs and an average of 75 to 80 cfs, although sustained flows of 100 cfs are common throughout much of the year. At 700 Springs hundreds, perhaps seven hundred springs fall out of the tall limestone bluffs above the river, and the, along with rock formations, vegetation, and birds, make this section of the South Llano especially pretty.

The south fork becomes accessible at the southernmost crossing of Highway 377, near the headwaters, northeast of Rock Springs. The narrow, rocky, upper portion is tricky to canoe. Farther down it widens out somewhat, with some long wide pools.

Joey Lin who guides on the south fork says any flies that work in central Texas will work on the South Fork of the Llano. Size 2, 4, and 6 baitfish patterns in chartreuse or a dark color, and poppers too, will do well on the south fork. Hellgrammites are abundant in the south fork's fast water where Guadalupe bass hold, patterns that represent them (Woolly Buggers will do) are a good choice. Guadalupe bass can get large on the Llano's south fork. In 2004, Joey's clients caught two that were 18 inches, and weighed about 2 1/2 pounds.

In 1997 and '98, four massive floods filled in many of the deep holes that were prime largemouth habitat. Largemouth bass will hold, cruise, and feed in shallow water, but they like deep water nearby, and since many of the big holes filled in there are not as many in the south fork as before. Of course, there is likely to still be some big largemouths in the remaining deep water, but fly-fishing long deep holes is a slow and exacting process that demands big flies fished deep and slowly. Historically, the south fork has not produced big largemouth like the main Llano, and devoting so much time on them is probably not worth your effort—probably.

Joey says that fishing is best on the lower river, so floating down to the state park or to the city park in Junction works well. On the lower part of the river, the left side is the deep side and where most of the bass hold. Plan to fish the lower part of the river in the afternoon when there is shade on the water, which is how it generally works anyway.

There is a small dam, on the south fork, slightly upstream of its confluence with the north fork in Junction called Junction Lake, that is accessible at Junction City Park. There are largemouth and sunfish in the lake. Floaters can take-out upstream of the dam, or put in downstream of it. Between Junction and FM 385, the Llano's flood plain is wide and flat and there are 19 miles of relatively slow-moving water with no major rapids. Yucca, cactus, mesquite, cedar and live oak line the banks, and there are a few limestone rock outcroppings.

Downstream of FM 385 the Llano gradually becomes swifter and more scenic as it flows through the Hill Country, but is still not a difficult river to float. The water quality improves and there are more sand and gravel bars than upstream. The section of river between FM 385 and US Highway 87 features some 200- to 300-foot red sandstone cliffs along the river.

This section of river does not have good access until it comes to county road 1871, southwest of Mason. This is known as White's Crossing, and from here to Llano is considered to be the river's prime fly-fishing water. Not much floating is done upstream of 1871 because it is over 20 miles between accesses, with many shallow stretches, and would require camping. You can launch at 1871 and float down to the next access, FM 2389, which is about two thirds of the way

Vegetation along the Llano River.

Hill Country fly-fishing guide Alvin Dedeaux on the Llano at HL Bluff.

through this 35-mile section, and known as the James River Crossing.

James River, a significant and fishable tributary, meets the Llano slightly upstream of the crossing. The James is 36 1/2 miles in length. The upper reaches are intermittent, but James Spring causes it to flow for 32 miles before it becomes intermittent again a few miles before it meets the Llano. Some people wade upstream to the Llano's confluence with the James River, but the James is not considered a navigable waterway. Landowners own the streambed, so you cannot legally stand and fish in it without permission. Technically, if you were to be floating on the water you would be considered legal, but there is no public place to launch upstream, and during normal flows no water downstream to come up on.

One of the largest bat nurseries in the country, the Eckert James River Bat Cave Preserve, is located near the James River. Approximately 4 million female Mexican free-tailed bats, most of them pregnant, arrive in May and inhabit the cave with their single pups through September. Each evening, as in Austin, the bats funnel out of the cave and spiral upward creating a spectacular show. The cave and surrounding property has been donated to the Texas Nature Conservancy by the Eckert family on the condition that it remain open to the public as it has

been for over a hundred years, (it does not include any river access).

Where 2389 crosses the Llano is an excellent access point. You can park and wade far up and downstream of the crossing, or launch a canoe or kayak. This is an official Mason County access with driving restrictions, designed to keep the longtime unofficial access legal after the state banned vehicles in streambeds in 2004. There is a five-mile speed limit within the 500-yard-long-and-250-yard-wide access that includes the state-owned gravel island within the streambed—no ATVs.

The float between James River Crossing and FM 1723 is a spectacular four miles of swift water and big pools that includes some awesome red sandstone cliffs. Alvin Dedeaux, a Hill Country guide, recognizable to many Texas fly-fishermen by his dreadlocks, took me down this section. Alvin floats in rafts which are pleasantly stable and bounce off rocks inconsequentially. The raft was more affected by wind than a canoe, but Alvin never seems to tire of rowing. It was an overcast day and the Guadalupe bass and sunfish eagerly hit our flies. The big largemouths were not so cooperative, but otherwise the action never stopped.

A geological area known as the Llano Uplift becomes evident at White's Crossing. The Uplift is an island of volcanic and metamorphic rock, principally pink and gray granite outcroppings, boulders and domes that protrude out of the surrounding sedimentary rock, of the Edwards Plateau. Its most prominent feature is Enchanted Rock, an enormous pink granite dome that glows at night. The uplift's granite rocks are deeply buried in the rest of Texas, but because the earth's crust is both thicker and lighter (imagine granite as light) than the surrounding area, the granite floats on the comparatively dense earth's mantle.

The Uplift is also a mineral zone, containing several rocks, mineral colored quartz, and a small amount of gold. The transition from the Edwards Plateau's red sandstone and white limestone begins upstream of the James River Crossing, and all three kinds of rocks and topography exist together for some distance in this picturesque section. The uplift continues approximately to the eastern border of Mason County near where Lake LBJ begins to back up the Llano.

From Highway 87 to the town of Llano is 30 miles of prime fishing water and splendid scenery. You can access the river at the Highway 87 bridge. The float from there to Castell is one of the best for scenery and fish, but you must be prepared to do 11 miles that includes many braided sections, steep drops, rock gardens, shallow riffles, and large pools where the

Raye Carrington rigging tackle and visiting with a guest at her bed & breakfast on the Llano.

ever-present upstream wind works against you. It can be a long tough float and there is no takeout point between. If you can catch the river up six inches to a foot, the float is much easier and faster.

Raye Carrington's fly-fishing-based, bed and breakfast of the same name, is two miles downstream from the Highway 87 bridge on Lower Willow Road. Raye offers rooms and cabins with a full breakfast cooked

by Raye's husband, David Jones (who took a guided trip with Raye in 2000, and never left), and private access to a good stretch of the river. You can show up at Raye's with nothing and no experience, or bring your own equipment, boat, and expertise. They will teach, guide, or shuttle you to other spots on the river with your own craft or with a kayak or canoe of theirs. Careful to maintain the inn's serene ambience, Raye and David do not allow put-ins, take-outs, or fishing access except for guests.

Even from Raye Carrington's it is a long float down to Castell. Raye can get floaters out at private property between her operation and Castell that is off limits to the public, so a less strenuous four-mile float is an option. Still, the float from Raye's to Castell is worth doing if you are up for a long day float and some paddling against the wind. The lack of access for so many miles makes for great fishing and a pleasant float.

I did this trip with guide Johnny Quiros, the other half of the Guides of Texas, and we saw only one other canoe. Fishing was great. We caught Guadalupes and sunfish all day long. In a deep run I hooked and broke off a strong fish that was almost surely a channel catfish. A bit farther downriver, a giant carp appeared under the canoe in shallow water. I handed my five-weight outfit to Johnny who had a better angle, he placed a chartreuse-and-white Clouser in front of the fish and the carp inhaled it. That was the only good look we got. Johnny and the carp engaged in a serious tugging contest that lasted about 10 minutes, before the fly pulled out. That carp was at least 20 pounds and looked to be 30.

This part of the river holds some big largemouths, but after spawning in April they drop into deep pools and are tough to catch. The Llano runs from west to east and the sun stays on these pools almost all day. Chances for a big bass are better on cloudy days, and in the few places where trees shade the water. The best chance for a big largemouth will be where there are trees, deep water, and current together.

The river is accessible downstream of Castell and several miles upstream of Llano (the town) at county roads 103 and 102. The 102 crossing, known as Scotts Crossing, is the best water, and parking is available on the midstream bedrock. This crossing is one that you do not want to attempt to ford when water is over the road. The road bed is a mixture of concrete and bedrock that rises and falls considerably. The area has a moonscape look with pink granite boulders, water, and not much else but the unrelenting sun. You can wade up or downstream a long way and still be in sight of the bridge. At the 103 crossing, known as Rice's Crossing, there is a place to park in the shade along the road. There is mostly flat water immediately up and downstream of the crossing.

At the town of Llano, there are several accesses to the river, a small dam and a shallow lake where trout are stocked in winter. You can park downstream of the dam and wade fish for a considerable distance down the river. Curiously, not many people fish the boulder-strewn pool below the dam, which has produced some big bass.

Downstream of Llano, the river flows approximately 20 miles before it is backed up by Lake LBJ. This section is mostly wide, shallow, and rocky. At normal flow it divides into several small streams and is a difficult float because of all the rocks, and there is no public place to take out for 19 miles. If the river is running well and you have permission to take out somewhere on private property, it would be worth fishing.

Highway 29 follows the river for about half this distance, and a pair of bald eagles has built a nest in sight of the road. In Kingsland there is a sandy access called the "Slab," which is a natural bedrock ford. If the water is not high you can cross between Highway 29 and 71. The Slab is most famous for the white bass and fishermen that congregate there in spring. You can wade upstream from the slab and catch Guadalupe bass. Shortly downstream of the Slab, Lake LBJ begins to backs up the river, if not before.

Guadalupe bass are the Llano's primary fly-rod fish. Most are less than 10 inches, but you will get some 12- 14-inch fish, and bigger ones on a good day. I have heard of three-pounders being caught, but Guadalupes that size are rare in the Llano and everywhere else. Largemouths up to five pounds, and bigger, inhabit the deep slow water of big pools. Due to their size, these streamlined river largemouths are highly prized. Whether they or the big Guadalupes are the Llano's prize fish is a good question.

The Guadalupe bass in the Llano are considered pure. No smallmouth have ever been stocked in the main river, although 6500 smallmouth were put in the north fork in 1958. Evidently that stocking did not take. Some have been put in the Highland Lakes, including LBJ, but they, or hybrids, have not, so far as anyone knows, gone up the river to upset the perfect combination of Guadalupes and largemouth in the Llano.

The same is not true of the Llano's native northern largemouths. There may be some pure northerns in the river, but most have been mixed with Florida strain largemouths from the reservoir. It is unclear whether Llano largemouths are now bigger because of their Florida genes.

Longears are the river's predominant sunfish, and there are also good numbers of bluegill and redear sunfish among others, including warmouth and green sunfish that take flies in the riffles like Guadalupes. In addition to bass and sunfish there are channel and flathead catfish, carp, and spotted gar in the Llano, and like rough fish in other clear Texas rivers, they will go for flies.

Llano River Guadalupe bass.

Rocky fast water downstream of Scotts Crossing near Llano, Texas.

There is a variety of forage fish in the Llano for bass to eat. Gizzard shad are an abundant food source for bass when they are small, but they eventually grow too large for anything but the flatheads to eat. About 10 species of shiners inhabit the Llano, of which red shiners are probably the most numerous. Male red shiners have bright red-orange fins and iridescent blue bodies during spawning season which can last from February through summer. Blacktail shiners are also present in good numbers, as are Texas shiners and stonerollers that eat algae off rocks. There are at least four darter species, plus young suckers, carp suckers, carp, and sunfish for the bass to eat. In addition to fish, the Llano holds hellgrammites, crawfish, several species of mayflies, caddisflies, and a few stonefly species. Grasshoppers are plentiful during warm weather.

The bass and sunfish rise well to hatches. David Jones recommends that fishermen use bigger versions of what is on the water—at least size 12. Turk's Tarantula, a rubber-legged trout fly with a deer-hair overwing that resembles a Muddler and suggests a variety of insects, including stoneflies and grasshoppers, is the one he and Raye use most often. Fished on top or in the film, Raye says that the bass are crazy for it. The Madame X is another good hopper pattern for the Llano, but most hopper patterns are good. David says that the more realistic a grasshopper fly is the less Llano bass like it, and therefore he recommends impressionistic flies. Size-six or eight cork-bodied poppers in chartreuse or black with rubber legs are good throughout the warm months, and sometimes in winter.

Chartreuse is a good all-round color for the Llano, and for streamers such as Clousers and wet flies.

A local pattern, the Llano River Bug, a chartreuse-and-black chenille nymph is a productive pattern. It is normally fished on a dead-drift, but a little action sometimes helps attract attention.

Raye and David prefer to fish dry flies and poppers on the Llano, but they say that guides depend heavily on olive and black Woolly Buggers, with bead heads and rubber legs, which catch channel catfish as well as bass. They should be fished with short irregular strips. Crawfish patterns are also a good bet. Hopper patterns, any of them, in size four and six are good from late spring into fall.

The Llano's clear water and wide-open character makes bass cautious. Once they become aware of your presence they are usually unwilling to hit, even though they may not move or otherwise indicate that they are spooked. Raye Carrington says bass are more cooperative at a distance, especially on clear days, and that a 40-foot cast is far more likely to produce a strike than one of 20 feet. A leader of at least nine feet also helps keep from spooking bass. Size 2X tippets are recommended, Guadalupe bass are not leader shy, and you may hook a big largemouth or catfish.

The Llano and its surrounding countryside looks and feels like quintessential Texas to me. It is uncommonly tranquil, and has so far escaped the second home and trendy resort development that is prevalent on many Hill Country river, due primarily to its relative isolation. With the exception of its final stretch, which is an arm of Lake LBJ and not far from Austin, the Llano is farther from large population centers than other Hill Country rivers, and there are no large reservoirs on the river that act as destinations.

6

Colorado River

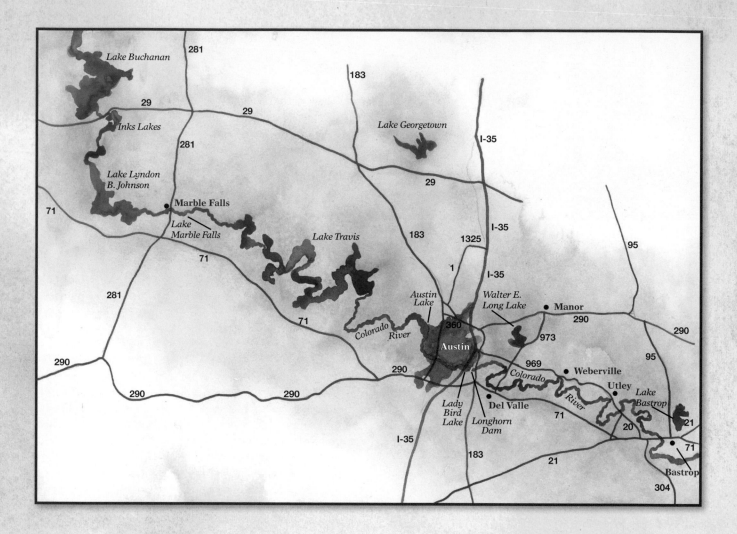

Texas' Colorado River does not start, end, or flow through the state of Colorado. Nor, is it red, like colorado in Spanish. It is unclear how the Colorado got its name. Various names were applied by Indians and the Spanish. Some historians say that its name was originally given to the Brazos River (Brazos de Dios or Arms of God), which is red in its headwaters, by Alonso De Leon in 1690. In the following years, the two rivers' names were often interchanged during the Spanish exploration, and eventually the name stuck to the Colorado instead of the Brazos.

The Colorado begins in salt-cedar-shaded, cattail-filled bogs east of Lamesa, in the west Texas county of Dawson. Some consider Rock Crusher (it is near

a quarry) otherwise known as Turner Springs, in TJF Draw to be its source, but there are many springs in many draws that contribute water to the river in the area, and the exact point of the Colorado's source is not a certainty. There are hundreds of miles of watershed and intermittent creek from which to pick a starting point. Texas Parks and Wildlife considers the Lamesa site the official beginning and that makes the river 600 miles long. Other estimates put the river's length at nearly 900 miles. It is the longest wholly contained river and watershed in Texas (the Brazos is longer but its watershed extends well into New Mexico).

From the west, it flows through rolling prairie, into the Hill Country, then continues through the coastal plain and finally into Matagorda Bay. The Colorado's upper portion is essentially a reservoir fishery due to its low or intermittent flow and limited access. Minnow species are the upper river's primary fish population, so fishermen aren't missing out on much. Though it does not have a sustained flow in its upper reaches, there is sufficient runoff to fill 7,820-acre Lake J. B. Thomas, 14,950-acre E. V. Spence, and 19,200-acre O. H. Ivie Lake during good years. J. B. Thomas is a turbid runoff reservoir, where fishing is poor. E. V. Spence has stripers and O. H. Ivie has smallmouths, both have white bass, crappie, catfish, and sunfish, and both have produced 14-pound largemouths in recent history. These reservoirs are on the main river, but there is also Lake Colorado City, Champion Creek Reservoir, Oak Creek Reservoir, plus the Old and New Ballinger lakes on its tributaries.

Under normal conditions, the Colorado's flow is sufficient to float a canoe at theHighway 277 bridge south of Bronte, although it doesn't look particularly inviting there. The Concho River, its first major tributary, and also a good fishing river, joins the Colorado in O. H. Ivie and from there on the river is probably fishable and floatable year round.

Downstream of O. H. Ivie, the Colorado is generally wide and shallow, flowing over limestone and gravel. It runs all year, but sections are extremely low in dry summers due to irrigation demands. At this point the Colorado begins to run out of the rolling prairie, and into the Hill Country where it flows through cedar-covered hills and scenic canyons with tall limestone bluffs.

The 26-mile section from Flat Rock, a large limestone slab near Bend, to Lake Buchannan is particularly scenic. This stretch includes Gorman Falls, a spectacular 60-foot waterfall on Gorman Creek where

it meets the Colorado. Since 1987 the falls has been contained within Colorado Bend State Park. The park offers access and primitive camping, a boat ramp and a fabulous, and well attended, white bass run in spring. The park is about nine miles upstream of the lake, and the river is navigable and wadable between the park's ramp and the lake.

Lake Buchanan is a 23,200-acre reservoir that holds largemouth, white, and striped bass, along with some Guadalupes, hybrids, and sunfish. It is the uppermost and largest of the "Highland Lakes," as they are called by the Lower Colorado River Authority (LCRA] which controls the Colorado from the Hill Country to the coast. Downstream of Lake Buchanan is Inks Lake, Lake LBJ, Lake Marble Falls, Lake Travis, and Lake Austin. Lake Austin is contained within Austin, as is the next and last of the Colorado River reservoirs, Lady Bird Lake which is owned and operated by the city of Austin. This series of reservoirs provides water, electricity, and flood control for Austin and the surrounding area. Buchanan is a holding dam, Inks, Starke (Lake Marble Falls), and Wirtz (Lake LBJ), are "pass through," or "run of the river" dams. These dams are designed to use upstream water releases for electricity generation, rather than releasing water on their own. Sudden water rises are not likely downstream of these dams, except for generator testing, and all LCRA dams have warning systems. Lake Travis, which produced the state-record Guadalupe bass, has a enormous flood pool intended to protect Austin. The combination of thin soil and steep slopes, with an extensive drainage that allows the Colorado to receive rainfall from hundreds of miles away, causes the National Weather Service to designate the Hill Country portion of the Colorado as "flash flood alley."

Lower Colorado River Guadalupe bass.

Larry Summers, who owned the famous Austin Angler fly shop, with Arrow, on Lady Bird Lake.

The rocky hill country where ranching and grazing are prevalent gives way to agricultural flat land in a matter of blocks in Austin. The Colorado abruptly changes from a rocky steep-sided Hill Country stream into a wide, comparatively lazy tree-lined river with dirt banks and a bottom of sand and gravel. Sandbars and access (the LCRA lists 23) are more numerous downstream of Austin, and bass are big and plentiful.

The Colorado between Austin and Smithville is a bass factory. The river's dirt banks are shaded by overhanging elm, willow, pecan, and sycamore with a profusion of water plants. All this habitat and structure combined with ample forage allows largemouth to grow quickly. Three-year-old largemouths are typically over 16 inches, and four year olds can be nearly 20 inches. Guadalupes of the same ages are 13 to 14 inches, and close to 15 inches respectively. This stretch of river has produced several ten-pound largemouths and three-pound Guadalupes, although there is some question as to whether the large Guadalupes are really hybrids. Smallmouth bass were stocked in the Colorado in 1980, 82, and 84, but not since.

There is also some question as to whether the lower Colorado's Guadalupes are really spotted bass which are native to that part of the river. TPWD simply called all non-largemouth bass Guadalupes in their electro shocking survey between Austin and LaGrange, but Guadalupes are considered to be mostly Hill Country fish, and the coastal plain part of the river is mostly spotted bass, with some overlap. Whatever the case, they are good-sized fish and great fun to catch.

Between Austin and LaGrange, gizzard shad are the most abundant prey species, followed by redbreast sunfish. The bass and catfish also eat threadfin shad, longear, green, and spotted sunfish, Rio Grande cichlid, logperch, blacktail, golden, and red shiners, crawfish, hellgrammites and other insects, and frogs. It is difficult to find a fly that doesn't look like something the fish will recognize as food.

Biologist Steve Magnelia says that the stretch between Longhorn Dam in Austin and Little Webberville Park has the highest number of largemouths in the lower river. Florida bass have never been stocked in the river, but they have been in the Highland Lakes and these fish have washed over Longhorn Dam. Downstream of the park, Guadalupe, or spotted bass, predominate. Steve also says that this part of the river is a world-class channel catfish fishery and they aggressively take flies. During a float between Little and Big Webberville parks with Bill Higdon, I hooked one in fast water on a Clouser that wrapped my line around some snags immediately and could not be extricated. Eventually it broke off, but it was an exciting experience. Steve says that the TPWD electro-shocking sampling turns up big numbers of 20- and 25-inch channels, and that they seem to prefer the fast water where aquatic invertebrates, such as insect larve, are most plentiful.

From May through October the Highland Lakes release water to be used for irrigation by downstream rice farmers. These water releases are often done at night, so the river is high and turbid in the morning. Under this scenario, morning flows may be one to three thousand cfs, but by afternoon the water will have dropped to the 300-700 cfs range. At the lower flow, pools and riffles develop, the water clears, and fishing gets good. Big rain will interrupt this cycle, but otherwise it is a semi-dependable scenario for a Texas river.

Bill Higdon, who guides on several Hill Country rivers, calls the Colorado "drift boat friendly," and compared to the bumping and grinding his boat does on the rocky Guadalupe, the Colorado is a smooth and quiet change. The river is also jet-boat friendly, and with sufficient flow, small outboards can be used. When water releases from the Highland Lakes subside, there may be long stretches of shallow water that may not float a motor boat. Canoes and kayaks are recommended for lower flows, but a drift boat could easily draft shallow stretches as well. There is plenty of heavy swift water and deep pools that cannot be waded, but between the pools, along sand and gravel bars, where the river splits, and in riffles you can park a boat and wade.

The Colorado holds bass all the way to the Gulf, but past Smithville bass numbers begin to drop off, and the river steadily becomes siltier. Near the coast it is brown.

★ 7

San Marcos River

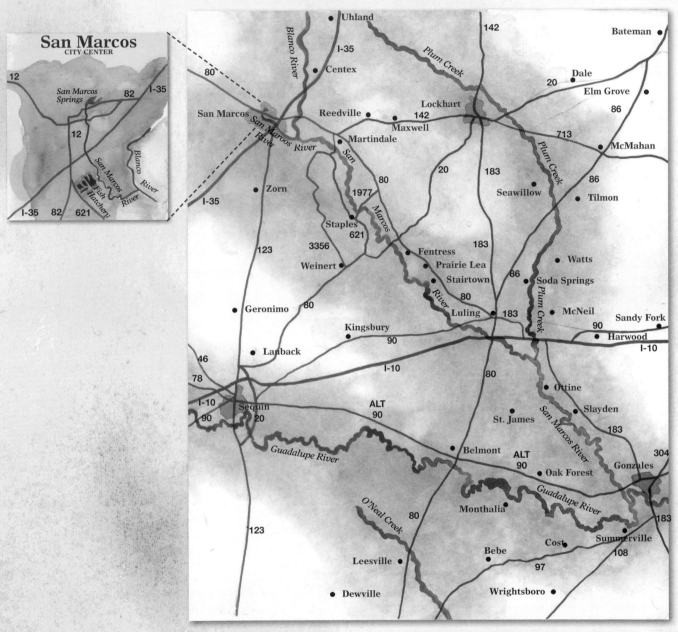

San Marcos
CITY CENTER

12
San Marcos Springs
82
I-35
12
San Marcos Fish Hatchery
Blanco River
I-35   82   621

Uhland
Blanco River
142
Bateman
I-35
Centex
Dale
20
Elm Grove
86
San Marcos
Reedville
Lockhart
142
Maxwell
713
McMahan
San Marcos River
Martindale
San
80
20
183
86
Zorn
1977
Seawillow
Tilmon
Staples
621
Marcos
183
Watts
3356
Fentress
Weinert
Prairie Lea
86
Soda Springs
Stairtown
McNeil
123
River
80
Sandy Fork
Geronimo
80
Luling
183
Plum Creek
90
Kingsbury
90
Harwood
I-10
Lanback
46
I-10
80
Ottine
78
ALT
90
Slayden
I-10
Sequin
St. James
San Marcos River
183
90
20
Belmont
ALT
90
Gonzales
304
Guadalupe River
Oak Forest
Guadalupe River
O'Neal Creek
80
Monthalia
183
123
Cost
Summerville
Bebe
108
Leesville
97
Dewville
Wrightsboro

he San Marcos (pronounced "San Markus" by Texans) begins as a series of strong springs producing a combined 150 million gallons of 72-degree water per day, averaging 180 cubic feet per second within the city limits of San Marcos—the second largest spring flow in Texas. The site is said to be the oldest continually inhabited place in North America. People have lived near the spring for about 12,000 years.

Initially the springs gushed with astonishing force from the base of cliffs and surged three and four feet,

or more, into the air from the stream bed. The 200 springs were inundated by a dam in 1854 and have remained so since. They can only be viewed (after a fashion) in an underwater theater and through glass-bottomed boats that carry tourists on the impoundment called Spring Lake. Entrance to Aquarena Park, as it is now known, is free.

In the 1900s a hotel was constructed on Spring Lake and the area was developed as a tourist attraction and resort called Aquarena Springs. There was a

Fly-Fishing guide Johnny Quiroz releasing a nice hybrid bass on the San Marcos River.

water show featuring Ralph the swimming and diving pig as headliner, accompanied by frolicking young "Aqumaids." Most people thought the park a wonderful family vacation spot and it was a sure revenue generator for the city—but not everyone felt that way.

In 1994, Southwest Texas University in San Marcos bought the springs and resort. The property continued to be operated as a theme park until 1996 when the university changed its focus to "educational and general uses," throwing out the pig, the Aquamaids, and the theme park rides after 30 years. Many people thought this was a long overdue improvement, but the city was not pleased about loosing $120,000 a year in revenue, numerous summer jobs, and an important tourist attraction. They would like to have it back, but the university is not selling.

Some would like to see the dam removed and the area returned to its natural state. The university is removing the numerous exotic plants and animals left over from the "theme park days," but does not intend to remove the dam. In the opinion of the university and the National Fish and Wildlife Service, the endangered Texas blind salamanders, San Marcos salamanders, fountain darters, San Marcos gambusia, and Texas wild rice, have adapted to the lake and would be worse off without it.

Due to the springs' strong flow, the San Marcos remains fishable through the summer and winter, its water temperature and flow varying little. The springs have never stopped flowing, so far as anyone knows. In the 1956 drought, the flow dropped to 46 cfs and Comal Springs in New Braunfels to the south ceased to flow at all. The Edwards Aquifer's level is measured by the J17 well at Ft. Sam Houston in San Antonio. At a level of 620 feet (where the top of the water is at that point) Comal Springs will cease flowing, but San Marcos Springs will not stop until the aquifer drops to 574 feet and that has not happened in recorded history.

From the springs and Spring Lake, the river flows through an area of city parks then goes under Interstate 35 and meets the Blanco about four miles from the springs. This upper portion is extremely clear and relatively slow and calm. Tubing is popular in the first two miles of river, but Cumming's Dam about four and one half miles downriver, backs up a long lake that effectively stops tubers. On Pecan Park Retreat's (a campground) website it states, "persons who have attempted to tube from town to Pecan Park have taken as long as twelve hours and were impossible to distinguish from white prunes once they got here." Though there is considerable current in the river, the relentless upstream wind that is so common on Texas rivers seriously compromises canoeing, so it is easy to imagine what a problem it would be for tubers.

The river is surprisingly fast, strong, deep, and sheltered by overhanging trees and bankside foliage. Non native elephant ear plants are thick along the bank providing cover for fish, and targets for flies. You can smack a fly on the big leaves and let it fall lightly and naturally to the surface. The river is so lush that it is jungle-like. There are big deep pools with undercut banks, fallen logs, and short rapids interspersed along the river's length. Gravel bars and places to wade are few.

The San Marcos produces huge largemouth for a stream. Its largemouth have Florida genes and can reach nearly ten pounds. TPWD has not stocked the Florida fish in the San Marcos. They have gotten into the river either by freelance stocking, overflowing private ponds (Florida-strain bass can be bought locally by individuals for their private water), or perhaps

Florida fish that were stocked in the Comal River have moved down the Guadalupe and up the San Marcos. Whatever the case, the river's huge deep pools and luxuriant cover are ideal for them, especially upstream of Staples. Native Guadalupe bass have been mixed with smallmouth. Few, if any, pure examples of either species exist, but occasional individuals exhibit a nearly pure look.

The uppermost and most popular portion of the river begins in the park at San Marcos. This area is easy to fish and there are plenty of small sunfish and bass, but bigger bass will be difficult to fool. There is a dam called Rio Visa in this section that backs up some deep water, and there is a nice, but busy stretch of fast water downstream of the dam. There is a slot in the dam that can be run, but you will get wet. Cummings Dam must be portaged.

Pecan Park, downstream of Cummings Dam, is a good place to put-in (there is a modest fee) for a fishing float. It is about four miles, or an easy half day, down to Sculls Crossing. The Blanco has already come into the San Marcos at this point so the river is quite strong. There are two named rapids in this section: Broken Bone and Cottonseed. Either can be run, but Cottonseed, where there is a broken concrete dam and a mass of rocks, is a good candidate to line if you don't wish to have your canoe or equipment banged up. Throughout this section you will see deep pools and short twisty rapids. Big sunfish are numerous and bass can be anywhere.

Another good float is from Martindale to Staples. You put-in at the crossing downstream of Martindale Dam and float to a point slightly upstream of Staples Dam. There is no parking at the Martindale end, you must unload the canoe and equipment then drive up the road a ways to park. There is ample parking at the crossing in Staples.

This section is a little longer and more open than the upper float. Some of the pools are lake-like, and require strenuous paddling against the wind to get through them. There are also several stretches of fast water, plenty of hybrid bass and sizable sunfish plus some big largemouth in this part of the San Marcos.

Downstream of Staples Dam, river traffic diminishes notably. Canoe rentals do not put clients on this stretch

Guide, client, and San Marcos hybrid bass.

Marcus Rodriguez keeps the canoe positioned while Diane Hicks casts a popper to bank side vegetation.

for fear of putting people in danger, and losing their canoes. From Staples downstream, the river becomes less clear due to runoff from dirt banks and tributary creeks. Johnny Quiroz and Marcus Rodriguez don't recommend this part of the river for beginners. After Staples, the river makes one abrupt turn after another, and the flow is deep and strong. Joey Lin considers this the most dangerous stretch of river in Texas.

Logs, stumps, and other debris pile up in these turns after floods. The river flows through these "strainers," but a canoe cannot. There will be a tight eddy in front, and if you do not know how to draw stroke out of it and ride the seam past, the bow will go into the eddy, cause the canoe to spin around and quite possibly flip. Or, you will run into the debris and also flip over, or be forced to get out on the log jam which is a deadly dangerous maneuver—one slip and you are in the water and under the log-jam.

Johnny and Marcus, who are highly skilled canoeists, like this part of the river for its isolation. They say hopper fishing is fabulous on this stretch when hot dry weather draws grasshoppers to the river's edge. If you wish to experience this part of the river, hire Johnny or Marcus, or Joey.

The San Marcos holds bass all the way to its confluence with the Guadalupe, but it gradually loses its clarity, beginning at Staples. Most people fish for catfish in the lower section, but according to Joey, if you fish big flies that make noise when they land and during the retrieve, you can catch bass in the murky water. Downstream of Luling, the river is usually muddy, though it can fish well for Guadalupe and spotted bass. Johnny and Marcus sometimes guide that stretch, but they generally do not recommend it. In addition to the murky water it is a 14-mile float to Palmetto State Park with much dead water, including a sizable backup from a dam upstream from the park.

Due to the strong spring water influence, the headwaters of the San Marcos remains warm through winter, cool in summer, and fishable all year. Past the confluence with the Blanco it is more seasonal— depending upon the Blanco's temperature, clarity, and flow, all of which can vary wildly. However, if the Blanco is running normally, the San Marcos will be a bit warmer in winter and cooler in summer than other Hill Country rivers. The river's abundant shade, combined with its substantial spring flow, makes it a prime river to fish in summer. How the San Marcos fishes in spring depends upon how cold and how fast the Blanco is flowing. The spring's influence keeps the river warmer than otherwise, and with some warm weather it warms up quickly.

The biggest problem with fishing the San Marcos in summer is tube traffic, which begins in late April and continues through September and into October if the weather stays warm. Tubes are to be expected where there are short stretches of river between accesses, particularly in the upper river, and especially in the headwaters portion in San Marcos. They are not so common in the river's lower sections, but Marcus says he has seen them as far down as Fentress.

★ 8

Blanco River

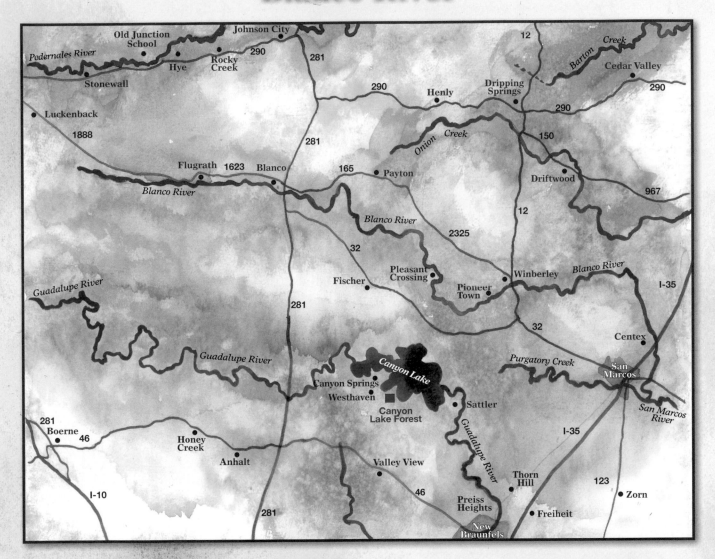

The Blanco is so named for the extensive white limestone along its banks and in its stream-bed—much of which is solid bedrock. It begins as a series of springs in northeast Kendall County and flows 87 miles to San Marcos where it meets the San Marcos River on the edge of town. It is not a large river, the productive stretch has a median flow of about 100 cfs. During dry spells, much of the river looks and fishes like a wet sidewalk, but there are dams, crossings, and an occasional fissure or channel in the bedrock where the water is deep. The Blanco falls out of the Edwards Plateau and onto the coastal plain at the Balcones Fault Line that parallels Interstate 35. As

the river runs out of the Hill Country the limestone is gradually replaced with clay and gravel, and the river turns south and takes on a classic pool-and-riffle configuration.

As with other Hill Country rivers, northern large-mouth and Guadalupe bass are native. A major stocking of smallmouth bass took place in 1977, and in 1980 there was a minor follow-up. Pure Guadalupe bass are rare, perhaps nonexistent in the Blanco except for the extreme upper portions where several small dams have inhibited the upstream progress of small-mouth and hybrids. The Blanco's hybrids are striking fish with charactcristics of both species, but they and the largemouth are finicky and spooky. In addition to bass, the Blanco holds channel and flathead catfish, gar, an array of sunfish, and Rio Grande perch.

The Blanco is not considered navigable by the state, so landowners own the riverbed in addition to the bank. There was, and may still be, a landowner or two who consider anyone in the river a trespasser and are not shy about pointing that out. Otherwise, if you access the river legally, stay between the banks, keep moving, and mind your manners no one is likely to complain.

There are three distinct sections of the Blanco. The uppermost section, from the headwaters to the bridge on Fischer Store Road, is extremely shallow and often dry in summer, except where dams and crossings pool water. There are a dozen or more dams in this section, varying from a few to 10-15 feet tall, that have been built to keep the river from going dry where people live, to water cattle, and to hold fish. Fish in this headwaters section are mostly small Guadalupe bass and sunfish with some catfish in the deeper water. The river can be accessed at the Blanco State Park in Blanco (trout are stocked there in winter). County Road 1623 follows the river upstream west of Blanco, and 1888 continues along the river to the upper headwaters. There are two accesses (one of which has public parking) along the road where taller dams hold enough water for a canoe or kickboat.

Kelly Watson, who lives and guides on the Blanco (among other rivers), regards the 30 miles of river from the Fischer Store Road Bridge, about ten miles upstream of Wimberley, to Dudley Johnson Park between Kyle and San Marcos as the most productive part of the river. The only access points in this middle section are Wayside Drive (aka the Slime Bridge) crossing, River Road upstream of Wimberley, and two county road crossings off Flite Acres Road, which is southeast of Wimberley off Ranch Road 12. These crossings may be described as suitable for car parking, but the local authorities and landowners say not. There are multiple signs to that effect and your car is almost certain to be towed if you leave it. All these points, including the Fischer Store Road Bridge, are drop-off accesses only.

The lack of parking in the Blanco's middle section impedes access, and reduces fishing pressure. The floats from Fischer Store Bridge to Wimberley, and from Wimberley down to the public access and take out at Dudley Johnson Park are both longer than ten miles and difficult to manage in one day. There are several

time-consuming portages around falls and chutes, and probably a good deal of dragging through the shallows, in addition to the time it takes to fish efficiently.

Camping between Fischer Bridge and Wimberley or between Wimberley and Dudley Moore Park would make these floats practical, but as you have no right to be on the river bed, islands, and certainly not on the river's banks, camping along the Blanco requires discretion. Kelly says that if you are away from houses and on an island you are probably OK, but landowner permission is the only sure way to camp lawfully. The easy way to solve the access and take-out problem is to stay at a bed & breakfast or cabin with river access, or hire a guide like Kelly who knows where to camp (and has permission) and how to fish. Kelly offers half-, full-, and two-day trips on the Blanco. He can also do a three-day trip, shuttles, or arrangs for take-outs and put-ins along the river or at his house

Rio Grande cichlid (usually called Rio Grande perch) from Blanco River.

in Kyle, located on a pretty and productive stretch of the river where it drops off the Balcones Fault.

Downstream of Dudley Johnson Park and Five Mile Dam, the Blanco is accessible in several places, but the price of that accessibility is fishing pressure. Big fish in this section are educated and wary. There is a fair chance of catching a nice bass in this stretch if you concentrate your efforts between the accesses, but it will be more challenging than it would be upstream. From I-35 to its confluence with the San Marcos, the river loses some but not too much of its clarity, the channel gets deeper, there are fewer rocks, and more mud and clay along the banks and on the bottom. The current slows somewhat but there are still chutes between the pools, and some of the pools are big and lake-like with lily pads.

Kelly says that the Blanco changes character at every bend, and from Fischer Bridge to Kyle you will see about 50 personality types. There are rock gardens, 400-foot-long bedrock flats, 20-foot-deep green pools, narrow chutes, wide-open areas, shaded banks, tall cliffs, dams and low-water crossings, in various sequences and configurations, all in close proximity.

Water depth and distance from accesses are the keys to success on the Blanco. The best fishing is in the bedrock stretch, where there are long stretches of water that are only inches deep (at best) in the summer, and anywhere you can find a degree of depth you will find bass. Depth is relative. Productive water doesn't have to be deep, only deeper than the surrounding water. Behind dams and in the deep pockets, Kelly recommends a sink-tip line for the larger bass that are often reluctant to come to the top. The Blanco is loaded with sunfish and small flies attract too many of them which will spook the bass. Kelly recommends using flies in the size 2-6 range.

Although the Blanco has multiple springs, including Jacob's Well that forms Cypress Creek in Wimberley, along its course it is more of a runoff stream than most other Hill Country rivers. Winter and summer water temperatures are less moderated by spring water and tend to reflect air temperatures. The Blanco can reach the 90s in summer and fall into the 40s during winter. If Blanco bass were pure smallmouth, they would be only slightly affected by a Texas winter, but as they are partly Guadalupe they are sensitive to cold.

Unlike purebred bass, the Blanco's hybrids do not all spawn at once when the moon and water temperature dictates. Depending upon how strong the smallmouth or Guadalupe influence is on their genes, Blanco hybrids may spawn from late February to the middle of May. Rather than having to closely time the spawn to get bass that are feeding heavily and less wary in the pre- and post-spawn patterns there is an extended window in which to capitalize. Weather and high water will also affect timing of the spawn. Largemouths in the Blanco spawn during the early spring, along with the first hybrid spawners.

In early spring, Kelly recommends sinking flies fished on sink-tip lines with a short heavy leader. He likes small lead-eyed crawfish patterns and Clousers, in addition to Cypert Minnows to which he adds a plastic curly tail. Whatever the pattern, it needs to be

Guide Kelly Watson sight-fishing for bass in a tailout on the Blanco River near Kyle, Texas.

weighted so it gets down fast where fish are holding in the deeper warmer water.

From late spring through summer the same patterns work, but they do not need so much weight. Warmer water moves fish out of the deep slow water, onto the shallow flats, and into fast water where bass begin to concentrate on top-water food such as frogs and grasshoppers. Grasshopper patterns, white and yellow poppers, and terrestrial patterns are effective from late spring till a major cold front or two comes through in late fall. Crawfish flies work late in the year, but they should be bigger, about two and one half inches, to match the growing crawfish that remain in the river. Until the weather gets really hot, bass, especially smallmouth and mainly smallmouth hybrids, will cruise the limestone flats even in bright sunshine hunting for crawfish and minnows.

When the weather and water cools significantly some time in October or, more likely, November, it is time to go back to the early spring techniques. A minor feeding phase will accompany the cooling water as the fish feel the urge to prepare for winter. Throughout winter, bass will be lethargic and holding in the deep pools. They are still catchable with a deeply fished fly, but winter fishing with flies on the Blanco is rarely a high percentage tactic. It is best when low water has concentrated the bass.

Walking and wading in the bedrock section is easy. As the river falls out of the Hill Country there are round rocks and cobble of various sizes that are hard on feet. Wear hard-soled shoes or you may get blisters that can develop into a painful plantars wart like I did, which lasted for a full two years even with medical treatment.

Devils River smallmouth habitat.

Sonora on Interstate 10, and Del Rio on the Mexican border. There is a store at Loma Alta on Highway 277 a few miles south of where Dolan Creek Road (twenty miles of gravel) cuts off to the Natural Area.

Springs provide 80% of the Devils' flow. The river flows intermittently till Pecan Springs enters upstream of Bakers Crossing on Highway 163, contributing enough additional water to sustain a constant flow. Gushing springs, mostly from the Hill Country side, continually add to the river's flow all the way to the lake. In the Natural Area, a series of springs called Finegan Springs gushes from the base of a limestone bluff beside the river. Downstream, Dolan Creek, fed by Dolan Springs, enters the river and swells the flow to a point that canoe dragging is not normally required from there on. Goodenough Spring, that flowed into the lower river and is now inundated by Lake Amistad, was once Texas' third strongest spring with an average flow of 137 cfs. The springs along the Devils have historically been considered drinkable— "historically" and "considered" are the key words here.

Even with all the obstacles and difficulties involved in fishing the Devils River, there are reasons to persevere—unspoiled natural beauty and big river bass. The TPWD record largemouth for the Devils is over eight pounds. That could be a fish caught in or near the reservoir that had Florida genes.

Largemouths in Amistad and the lower river have Florida genes, but above Dolan Falls they are still pure northerns. The state is raising and then releasing the more aggressive northern largemouths into the reservoir to increase the native genes in Amistad's fish thereby producing a large, but catchable bass.

Smallmouth are the Devils' predominate bass. TPWD did a survey in 2000 where they floated the river from Bakers Crossing to Paffords Crossing (a private crossing where there is a weir and cable across the river) near where Amistad backs up the river. They caught 37 largemouth ranging from six to almost 20 inches, and averaging 10 inches. The trip also produced 489 smallmouth from five to slightly over 21 inches, which would have probably weighed five or six pounds, that averaged about nine inches. These fish were caught on rod and reel during a three-day float, which is uncomfortably fast for that many miles.

Typical of the species, smallmouth tend to hold in the river's faster sections, and largemouths are more prominent in slower water. There are no Guadalupes in the Devils. Channel and flathead catfish live in the deep pools. Redear and longear sunfish are the most abundant of a variety of sunfish in the Devils. They, minnows, and crawfish are the major forage for the bass. Near the reservoir, shad are present, and there is a spring white bass run.

Other Hill Country Rivers
Medina, Sabinal, Frio and Nueces Rivers

In the south-central part of the Hill Country west of San Antonio is a pocket of rugged hills, canyons, and some of the Edwards Plateau's highest points. Air-clear streams, fed by springs flow south out of the Hill Country through tunnels of ancient cypress trees into the south Texas brush land. These rivers, including the Medina, Sabinal, Frio, and upper Nueces, are considered to be the Hill Country's gems by many. Floods in the late 90s washed gravel into many of the holes, so they do not fish so well as before.

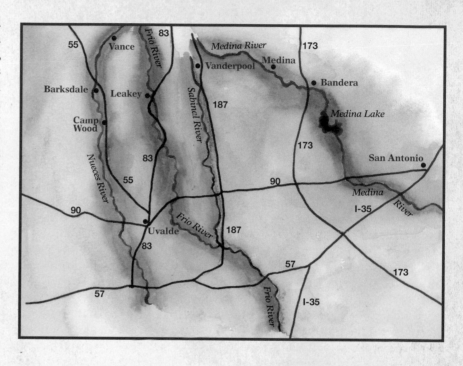

These streams hold opportunistic fish that are waiting for something to fall into the water. Fishing for them is not, according to Joey Lin, "rocket science." If you show them a fly that looks edible, present it properly, and don't spook them, they are probably going to take it. The guy in front of the canoe gets one or two shots, then the fish scatter and you may as well move on.

The Medina River, short by Texas standards, begins in northwest Bandera County and flows approximately 116 miles before meeting the San Antonio River southeast of San Antonio. The upper portion runs strongly because of springs, but downstream of Medina Lake it is often too low to float. In terms of safety and access, the stretch between Medina and Bandera is a good float.

The Medina flows through a constricted limestone and cypress corridor. Flood water has nowhere to go but through the river's narrow course, and flows approaching 200 cfs make it a technical challenge with standing waves, sharp turns, and dangerous volumes of water within an enclosed space. Numerous springs feed the Medina along its course keeping it cool and clear. Joey, who guides fly-fishermen there, says, "You can see a dime on the bottom in 12 feet of water, and every fish in a pool will scatter if you bang the side of the canoe." Sediment stirred up by wading upstream of holding water will also put fish down. Despite the floods it is still well worth fishing when flowing well.

Tube traffic is essentially relegated to the lower parts when the flow is good. Two weeks of dry summer weather and it will drop to 70 cfs which makes tubing tough.

The upper Sabinal flows through Lost Maples State Natural Area, where there is a large isolated stand of bigtooth maple trees. In fall, when conditions are right, these trees turn a brilliant red, and because there is so little fall color in Texas, the park is extremely popular that time of year. It has a color watch website. This part of the Sabinal and its tributary Can Creek, is a designated Guadalupe bass refuge. No smallmouth genes have touched the bass in this little river. The Sabinal is too small for serious floating.

The Frio (Spanish for cold) River is also similar to the Medina. The upper part flows well, but at Con Can it becomes intermittent. The Frio gets a great deal of tube traffic, but offers interesting fishing for bass and sunfish.

The Nueces River (pronounced "new aces") is reputed to be the clearest river in the state. Fishing is done mostly downstream of Vance where the river flows continually and access is better than upstream. There are a few big largemouths and many Guadalupes in the Nueces, along with sunfish and Rio Grande perch.

East Texas Rivers

16-17

Red River and Texoma Reservoir

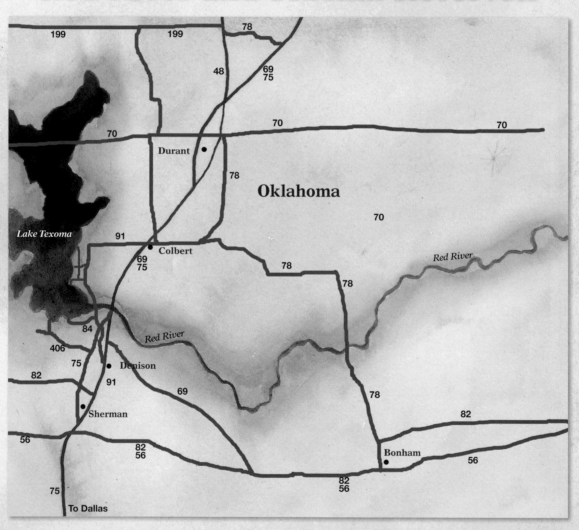

Forming the border between Texas and Oklahoma is the Red River. Upstream of Texoma Reservoir the river lives up to its name, but the silt falls out in Texoma. It is a good lake for largemouth, and a great lake for stripped bass. The river downstream of Texoma also has a strong striped bass run in spring. Stripers hold in pools downstream, then when generation starts, move up to the dam. There is large public access downstream of the dam on both sides of the river where you have a chance of catching a striper on a fly, but you will be competing with fishermen using heavy-duty spinning rods, with jigs and plugs that can cast the proverbial "country mile." Air boats are widely used on the river, and with one you can fish the pools downstream of the dam that cannot be reached by other means, and you will have a much better chance of success.

Sabine River, Village Creek & Neches River

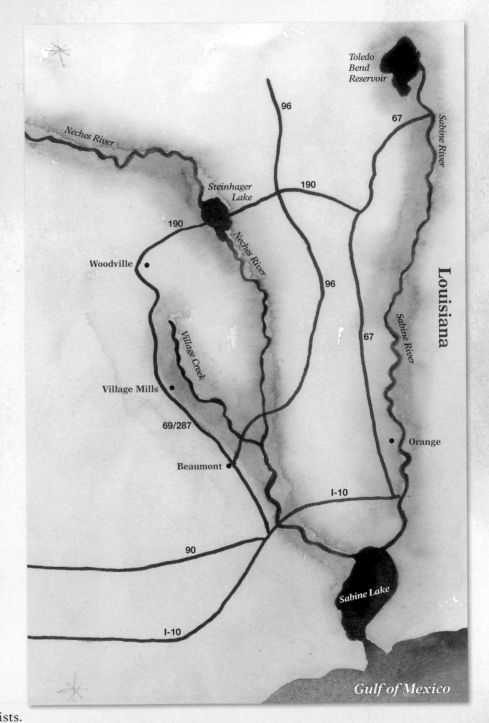

In addition to the lakes in east Texas there are several rivers that offer excellent fly-fishing for bass and sunfish. East Texas rivers and streams are not so fast or clear as those in the Hill Country, and may be tea-stained by the pines, but they have a certain charm and are not fly-fished much. In particular, the rivers that flow through the Big Thicket National Preserve, the remnants of a once-vast forest of pines, hardwoods, and cypress where eastern hardwood forests, the Gulf coastal plains, and Mid-west prairies meet, are scenic and quite remote in places. The resulting mix of regions sustained a diverse selection of plant and animal life that is impressive even for Texas.

The Neches River and Village Creek each flow through sections of the Big Thicket Preserve. The Neches is over 400 miles in length, flowing mostly through dense woods. A 56-mile stretch downstream of B.A. Stienhagen Reservoir is a designated Big Thicket river corridor. The river is relatively clear near the reservoir, but becomes more murky as it flows toward Beaumont and eventually into Sabine Lake. It is predominantly a largemouth stream. Village Creek, a tributary of the Neches, is a popular and scenic canoe stream. There are white sand bars and enough largemouth bass to be interesting for fly-fishermen. Both rivers are suitable for novice canoeists.

The Sabine River, which divides Texas from Louisiana, provides good fishing for largemouth bass, plus a chance for stripers and various pan- and sunfish. The section between Toledo Bend Reservoir and Orange, Texas is more bassy than the river upstream of Toledo Bend which is primarily a catfish river.

The Texas Coast

Above: Ladyfish.

Right: South Texas Sunset.

Below: Captain Scott Sparrow's VIP Poppers.

CAPTAIN SCOTT SPARROW

CAPTAIN SCOTT SPARROW

CAPTAIN SCOTT SPARROW

CAPTAIN SCOTT SPARROW

Above: Laughing gull rides the ferry from Galveston Island to the Bolivar Peninsula.

Left: Big redfish splashing in shallow flats water.

Texas flats can seam endless.

There are 367 miles of Gulf coastline in Texas, and according to the Texas General Land Offices' Texas Beach & Bay Access Guide, 3,300 of bay shoreline, including islands. From the Louisiana border to Mexico, barrier islands protect almost all the mainland and bay systems. The Texas coastal plain is flat as land can be, and saltwater bays behind the barrier islands are shallow with expansive flats that are ideal for fly-fishing. Fishable flats are considered to be between six inches and three feet deep. The bays themselves have maximum depths of 2 to 20 feet with a great deal of 3- to 8-foot water, except where the shipping lanes and the Intracoastal Waterway (ICWW) have been dredged through them.

The Intracoastal Waterway is a toll-free canal built by the U. S. Army Corps of Engineers that runs from the Calooshatchee River in Florida to Brownsville, Texas. All but a 140-mile section in Florida is protected from the open Gulf of Mexico. In total, it runs 1,209 miles and is maintained to be 100 feet wide and nine feet deep. Fish in Texas' shallow bays are fond of its depth for safety and warmth during cold snaps.

Water along the Texas coast is not so clear as on the East and West coasts. All Texas rivers end in the Gulf and run through thick soil in their lower sections where they pick up substantial mud and silt under normal flows and dump massive amounts of dingy chocolate water into the bays when floods occur. The fresh water also brings phytoplankton into the bays which makes the water cloudy, but rich. Where there are fewer freshwater inflows, as with the Upper and Lower Laguna Madres, the water is clear and extra salty, or hypersaline. Offshore, the Gulf of Mexico is blue green. Wind and tides sometimes bring that water close to the shore and into the jetties, but not to the backs of the bays. When that happens, it brings offshore species within reach of shore and jetty fishermen.

There are eight coastal bay systems: Sabine Lake which Texas shares with Louisiana, then Galveston, East Matagorda, San Antonio, Aransas, Corpus Christi, Upper Laguna Madre, and Lower Laguna Madre, the southernmost. The Texas Coast is divided into upper, middle, and lower sections for reference. The divisions are not precise, but the Texas Parks and Wildlife Department considers the upper portion to begin at the Louisiana border, and includes Sabine Lake and Galveston Bays. The middle coast contains Matagorda, San Antonio, and Aransas Bays. The south coast includes Corpus Christi Bay and the Upper and Lower Laguna Madre. Each bay system includes sub-bays, some of which are extensive.

Coastal History

Krankawa Indians were the original inhabitants of the Texas Coast. They were a nomadic conglomeration of several sub-tribes that lived from Galveston Island to Corpus Christi and shared a common language and customs. They moved back and forth from the barrier islands to the mainland in dugout canoes as seasonal fishing and foraging dictated. The men were said to be seven feet tall and wore few if any clothes. Krankawa women wore skirts of Spanish moss or animal skins. Both sexes smeared alligator or shark grease mixed with mud on their tattooed and pierced bodies to ward off mosquitoes. It is difficult to imagine anyone smelling nice anywhere in Texas in those days, but the Krankawas apparently out-smelled the European(s) by a wide margin. That, in addition to their menacing looks, ferocious nature, and cannibalistic tendencies made them rather unpopular. They also had the nerve to resist European customs and religion—though the Spanish built missions to convert them. After 300 years of contact with Europeans, the Krankawas still retained their own customs and way of life. Many died of European diseases, but the last band of Krankawas was annihilated by Texas soldiers in 1858 near Rio Grande City.

The Texas coast was also frequented by pirates, most notably Jean Lafitte and his brother Pierre. Jean Lafitte managed to get mixed up in the politics of Spain, Mexico, and the United States. He was also involved in the Mexican and American revolutions. After helping the Continental Army at the Battle of New Orleans, Lafitte thought he should be pardoned for his extensive piracy.

When this did not happen, Lafitte left New Orleans and Louisiana, and established a pirate colony that became the center for his operations on Galveston Island in 1817. Lafitte, his associates and other pirates, and families in some cases, remained at Galveston till 1821 when, after Lafitte kept postponing his departure, President Madison sent warships and made it clear that Lafitte was to leave or be blown to pieces. That night, Lafitte set fire to the settlement called Campeche, and in the morning he and his ships were gone. Jean Lafitte, know as the "gentleman pirate," and who called himself a corsair or privateer, never a pirate, went to an island off Yucatan and continued his operations till his death in 1825. By other accounts, he went to North Carolina then disappeared, and perhaps fought with Boliver's rebels in South America. Whatever the case, Jean Lafitte was, to say the least, a colorful character of Texas history.

Spanish treasure ships sailing home from Mexico were the main target of pirates such as the Lafittes. It is legend that a large treasure is buried on Mustang Island beneath a dagger Lafitte stuck in the sand. Ships with treasure regularly wrecked on the coast as well. In the 50s, while cutting the Mansfield Ship Channel through Padre Island, the dredge struck a Spanish Galleon buried in the sand and threw wood shards mixed with silver coins all over the sand. It was one of three galleons that were eventually uncovered there.

Now the Texas Coast is a blend of industry and recreation. Oil and natural gas is pumped, piped, and shipped from and along the coast and far out into the Gulf. There are refineries, commercial fishing and shrimp boats, and all manner of commerce in addition to sport fishing and tourism. The coast is busy near the population centers. The beaches draw swimmers, surfers, fishermen, and tourists all summer long. In winter, people forsake the frozen north and escape to Texas. They are known by locals as "winter Texans." The joke used to be that winter Texans came with one shirt and a 20-dollar bill and never changed either. That element is still well represented, but modern winter Texans are now likely to arrive in a $250,000 motor home, but they are still just as cheap.

Guides who take customers out in salt water are called captains. To obtain a captain's license a guide must pass four separate tests: charting, rules of the road (markers, lights, etc.), safety, and general navigation.

Saltwater Equipment

An eight-weight and an eleven- or twelve-weight outfit will handle all the saltwater fish anglers fish for under all normal conditions. When there is no wind on the flats, some fly-fishermen may use a seven- or perhaps a six-weight outfit for smaller redfish, seatrout, Spanish mackerel, ladyfish, and other smallish saltwater species. Others prefer a 10- or 11-weight to a twelve, for big saltwater fish, but you are safe with an eight and 12.

Modern fly equipment needs little or no special care and maintenance when used in salt water. Most reels are anodized, and rinsing it and the rod with fresh water after a day of fishing will normally suffice. It is a good idea to occasionally pull the line out and rinse it and to lubricate the reel's spindle.

Regular fly line goes limp when the weather and water gets really hot like it does in Texas. Scientific Anglers Bonefish Taper or a similar line designed to remain stiff in hot water, load quickly, and minimize the effects of wind, will greatly enhance your flats casting.

Special flats boots are recommended. Some styles use Velcro or side zippers, and they are easy to put on and take off. Boots that tie, like Simms' Flats Sneakers, present additional security when wading mucky bottoms,that threaten to suck the boots off your feet.

The summer sun, wind, salt, heat, and humidity at the coast will kill you if you are not prepared. Don't expect any shade on the coast, and certainly not on the flats. A lightweight breathable broad-brimmed hat that covers your ears and neck is a must. No hat that fits this criteria is stylish, so don't waste time looking for one that is. Lightweight long-sleeved shirts and long pants (zip off pants/shorts are popular), some of which now have SPF ratings, dark polarized sunglasses for strong sun, sungloves, and sunscreen complete the protection system. Early and late or on overcast days, lighter amber glasses, which are better for fish sighting, can be used. Under the same conditions, short sleeves and shorts are OK, but even with cloud cover you will need sunscreen to stay out all day.

In terms of hydration, there is not substitute for water during a Texas summer. Soda and beer are counterproductive, but if you consciously keep drinking water you will stay comfortable and energetic. Don't wait to get thirsty or feel fatigued from dehydration—it will be too late.

Sunrise over backwater on Texas coast.

Texas Saltwater Fish

A pod of red drum feeding on shrimp with an opportunistic laughing gull hovering above.

Red Drum

Normally called "redfish," or "reds," red drum are the Texas flats fly-fisherman's staple. Both red drum and spotted seatrout are highly sought-after species along the Texas Coast, but red drum are probably the most popular with fly-fishermen because they are more numerous than seatrout on the flats where fly-fishermen tend to fish most. Red drum are in the croaker family and they, like the other croakers, can make croaking and drumming noises with their air bladder.

Redfish inhabit bays and feed on the flats until they grow to about 30 inches between their third and fourth year. At that point, they move out into the Gulf and spawn, normally do not return to the bays, and are then referred to as "bull" reds though the really big ones are always old females. Their eggs hatch within 24 hours and the tide carries the young redfish, or eggs, back into bays where the larvae seek

quiet grassy water with a muddy bottom. Juveniles eat small crabs, shrimp, and marine worms working up to larger crabs and worms, and small fish as they grow.

Redfish are eager feeders and take flies with enthusiasm. They are not leader shy and because they are looking down when feeding they may come close to a stationary angler and may possibly be approached by a stealthy one—this is not the case when they are cruising. Redfish are highly sensitive to vibration, such as clumsy footsteps on a boat deck, or awkward splashy wading.

After moving to Texas, my first experience with them was in the Lower Laguna Madre with veteran Captain Eric Glass. It was a breezy, choppy morning and I was far from recovered from the previous day's brutal 544-mile drive from the Dallas area to Brownsville, against the wind, and with minimal sleep. Both the deck and I were unsteady. Eric was poling and pointing out redfish tails and I was consistently losing my balance. Every time I caught myself with a hard footfall, I spooked the fish, and Eric probably winced, even though he said nothing after a couple of times. Fortunately, it was spring when the redfish feed most actively and the overcast sky kept them on the flats longer than they would stay on a bright day. The chop made them less spooky. No matter how many I spooked there was always another to cast to, and if I put the fly where the fish could see it I got a strike. We caught and released 3- 7-pound redfish all

Captain Scott Sparrow with a nice seatrout.

76

Captian Eric Glass with a nice redfish.

morning and into the afternoon. We could have filled the boat with them.

Redfish can live anywhere. They are found in all the Texas bays, the Gulf of Mexico, in five freshwater lakes, and sometimes even run up rivers. There are good populations of them all along the coast, in bays, in the surf, and off shore around structures like the drilling rigs. Areas where there are many passes between the Gulf and the bays where fish and eggs or larvae can move back and forth are especially conducive to redfish reproduction, and consequently good fishing. Redfish are long lived and have been known to exceed 90 pounds, but most fly-caught fish are two to six pounds. In Texas they have been caught up to almost 60 pounds with rod and reel, and close to 30 with fly gear.

Shrimp, crabs, and small fish are redfish staples and flies for them generally fall into one of these categories. On the flats, small poppers work well, and where the water is shallow and sea grass thick, they afford a distinct advantage because they float above the grass. Redfish mouths are angled downward so they can grub for and capture food on the bottom. They have to raise their heads partly out of the water to hit surface lures, which makes for a distinctive surface take. Once hooked, even an average-sized redfish will make two or three runs into the backing.

Now abundant in Texas, red drum were at risk in the 70s and early 80s due to intense commercial netting and unregulated sport fishing. With no lim-

its, sport fishermen could take all the redfish and seatrout they wanted. Some sport fishermen measured their catch not by numbers or pounds, but by how many 48-quart ice chests they could fill. The sportfishing catch, huge at it was, still paled in comparison to that of the netters. In 1977, a group of sportsmen met at Rudy Grigar's tackle shop in Houston and formed the Gulf Coast Conservation Association (GCCA). With 40 original members, the GCCA began pushing to save the redfish. In 1979, a bill was passed that limited sport fishermen's catch to ten redfish and 20 seatrout per day. In 1981, after years of an ugly "redfish war," between commercial fishermen and conservationists, the "redfish bill," as it was known was passed and redfish were granted gamefish status. Redfish are prolific spawners and with protection from commercial fishing, limits for sport fishermen, and some help from hatcheries, they began to recover nicely. Now the GCCA has dropped the Gulf and is the CCA, promoting conservation from Texas to Maine. The limit is three 20- to 28-inch redfish per day, and one bigger one per year. Catch-and-release fishing is now common, (but certainly not standard), especially among fly-fishermen.

Spotted Seatrout

While redfish are the main flats fish, another croaker, spotted seatrout, are also present, and they tend to be larger than ones in the bays' deeper water. Most seatrout on the flats are 18 inches or larger and are considered to be more difficult that redfish to catch. Where there are channels, such as the Intracoastal Waterway, seatrout will be more numerous than redfish, but smaller. Small seatrout are easier to catch than redfish, but big ones are more challenging.

Seatrout—also called speckled trout, trout, or specs—are pursued by all kinds of fishermen everywhere on the coast. They are the most landed saltwater fish in Texas. Seatrout, like redfish, are tasty and fun to catch. As with redfish, spotted seatrout were granted gamefish status in by the redfish bill in 1981. A major rallying point for the GCCA came in 1978 when 200,000 pounds of seatrout all packed into the Houston Ship Channel during a freeze were effortlessly netted by shrimp boats.

Seatrout spawning takes place at night all over bays, but grass flats, if available, are preferred for spawning because they will provide the young fish with food and shelter. Spotted seatrout reach maturity at 13 inches, and grow to about 15 inches in their second year. Most are less than 20 inches, and a 25-inch seatrout is considered to be a trophy. Females, called "sows," grow much larger than males. Seatrout over 15 pounds have been caught in Texas, and that fish, which was over 37 inches, was caught on a fly. They occasionally jump at the moment they are hooked, but otherwise shake their heads and splash on the surface attempting to throw the hook.

Seatrout, like redfish, feed on shrimp, crabs, and small fish—mostly mullet. Those over 20 inches feed almost exclusively on fish. They are toothy aggressive fish with a slightly bloodthirsty reputation. It is said that they can consume prey up to half their size. Seatrout have two prominent teeth on the top of their mouths, and if you attempt to land one by sticking your hand in its mouth it will stick you and you will bleed. Grasp them gently behind the gills unless you have a Boga Grip and can lip them. It was once common to hear people say, "a caught trout is a dead trout," many fishermen probably believed that, but a more convenient excuse to justify keeping seatrout could not be contrived. Trout can be released, but they are a bit fragile.

.

Black Drum

Black drum are not considered game fish and are not pursued by sport fishermen nearly to the extent of their croaker cousins, the redfish and seatrout. They are a great deal bigger and more compact than red drum, and have black vertical stripes. Black drum are less frequent on the flats, extremely spooky, and are less sensitive to cold water than red drum or seatrout. They have barbells on their chins to help find food by feel and smell. Young black drum eat marine worms, small shrimp, crabs, and fish. Big drum also eat algae and mollusks, which they sometimes root out while tailing, forming small craters in the bottom called "drum noodles." Black drum have no canine teeth like seatrout, but have strong teeth in their throats with which they can crush mollusks and crabs.

Black drum can live in fresh water, water twice as salty as the ocean, shallow flats, and in Gulf water more than a 100 feet deep, and everywhere in between. They spawn in bays, the Gulf, or in passes by randomly releasing eggs in late winter and early spring, with additional spawning in summer.

During summer, there are schools of drum up to about four pounds on the flats. In clear water they can be sight-casted to if you can get close enough. Otherwise, watch for patches of muddy water that have been stirred up by their feeding activity. In winter, large and small black drum frequent deeper water, channels, and the Gulf surf.

Going out for Tarpon

Port Aransas Tex

Boats racing out to meet the tarpon.

and baitfish to pass over them. Flounders effectively camouflage themselves to match the bottom. It has been documented that they can duplicate the pattern on a checker board. In pursuit of prey, they sometimes jump, effecting what is known as the "flounder flop."

Southern flounder spend most of their time in the bays and on the flats, but leave in fall to spawn in the Gulf. The fry move back into the bays where they spend two years and grow to about 14 inches before they spawn. The state record is a 13-pound fish from Sabine Lake, and the fly-fishing record is a five-pounder from Galveston Bay that hit a Clouser.

Baitfish patterns fished along the bottom are standard for this species. Flounder are not classed as game fish and gigging them (called floundering) at night while wading or poling a boat with a lantern is a popular method for taking them.

Tarpon

Texas was once teeming with tarpon, and fishing for them was big business for local guides. Tarpon numbers, or at least the numbers caught, peaked in the teens, 20s, and 30s, but in the late 50s they began to decline. One year in the late 60s, they were gone. There were several factors that contributed, although no one is in complete agreement about them or virtually anything else concerning this ancient and mysterious species.

During the 50s, automobile traffic increased significantly on the beaches and that meant many more tarpon were caught and kept. At the same time, motors became common on boats. When the tarpon fishery was

Texas tarpon from the good old days.

Thirty- to 40-pound black drum are a possibility, specimens over 80 have been taken with rod and reel from the Gulf in Texas and nearly 20 with fly equipment from Lower Laguna Madre. Black drum are a staple of the commercial fishing industry, and those under five pounds are considered good to eat. The largest on record weighed 146 pounds. Black drum occur from the New York to the Mexican coast, but are most numerous from Corpus Christi to the Mexican border. They are not aggressive fly-takers, but will sometimes strike flies laid on the bottom and have been known to chase and catch gold spoon flies.

Southern Flounder

The largest and most common species of Texas flounders, the southern flounder is found in bays and along or near the coast. They are, like other flatfish, funny looking with both their eyes on one side—with southern flounder the left side is always the up side, but that is not true of all flounder species—of their head and are exceedingly good to eat. Flounder lie motionless on the bottom and wait for unsuspecting shrimp

Fat snook caught from South Padre jetty.

at its peak, guides rowed their clients, severely limiting their coverage. It is also said that the tarpon disappeared at the same time as the brown pelicans, and that was related to agricultural runoff, DDT in particular.

In the 60s, farms increased in size and mechanized farming really got going. Commercial gill netting of fish began, including tarpon, for fish-processing plants in Mexico to be made into fish meal for pet food. Back then, tarpon spent the winter around Tampico, Mexico and the summers in Texas, which is different from how tarpon range today. All these factors came together to reduce tarpon numbers, or so it is thought. No one really knows, nor can they prove exactly what happened. There are some who claimed the tarpon never really disappeared, but for some reason people couldn't catch them.

They is no doubt that tarpon are the fly-fishing prize of the Texas coast, but their way of life is still a mystery, with more theories and conjecture than facts. What is known is that they like warm water and appear from June through October along the Texas coast, with August and September being the most productive months. As the water cools they leave, sooner in the north and later in the south. Tarpon feed mainly on fish and shrimp, and tarpon flies generally are imitations of one or the other. Flies called Tarpon Bunnies, a combination of rabbit strip and feathers tied on a 1/0 - 3/0 circle hooks and attached to an 80-pound shock leader to protect against their sharp gill plates are stand-bys, and a variety of other big baitfish flies will work. They can be spotted rolling and gulping air, and by watching for feeding birds and fleeing baitfish.

It is not certain where tarpon spawn. It was thought for some time that they spawned in bays, but now the evidence appears to say they move from the bays immediately, before spawning, and spawn offshore in depths of 150 to 200 feet. Tarpon larvae, an elongated transparent type similar to an eel larva, has been found offshore in the Gulf, and it seems unlikely such small larvae could make it out 20 miles into the Gulf from back in the bays.

Ten- to 12-weight outfits are standard for tarpon, with 10 being on the light side. An eight-weight is essentially useless on a tarpon of any size, and such a fish would not be easy to handle with a big rod. Several things must come together and be just right even to hook one—and that is unlikely enough—but landing one is an extraordinary challenge. Their mouths are hard and hooks don't stick well, they are incredibly strong and jump repeatedly. Eric Glass said he landed the fifteenth one he hooked, and that may be about the odds—for an expert.

Snook

There are two species of snook in Texas. One, the common snook otherwise known as roballo or saltwater pike, is the largest. Most common snook caught in Texas are less then 10 pounds. The rod-and-reel record common snook is a 57-pound fish caught in 1937. The fly-fishing record is a comparatively new and small, 5.56 pounds caught in 1999, but larger ones have been caught and released by fly-fishermen.

Like tarpon, they were once plentiful, and were also taken commercially in the past. Snook can live in fresh or salt water, and sometimes move far up rivers. They are found mostly in the Lower Laguna Madre, around South Padre Island, and in the Brownsville Ship Channel in far south Texas, but they do show up north of there from time to time. Snook are warm-water fish, and quite sensitive to water temperature. Biologist Rebecca Hensley says, "If you throw an ice cube in the water, they will die."

Snook are attracted to structure, such as mangrove roots, bridges, jetties, and docks. Fishing for them is similar to fishing for freshwater bass. Streamer fly patterns that resemble baitfish such as mullet, pinfish, menhaden and silversides are a good bet.

The other species, called a fat snook, is smaller, thicker, and more abundant. They are frequently caught off jetties, and like common snook they are fished for much like largemouth bass. There are two species of fat snook, big scale and little scale. Fat snook rarely exceed 20 inches.

Crevalle Jack

Called "jack crevalle" or "jacks," these aggressive, blunt-nosed fish are known for savagely slashing into schools of baitfish from all sides. During these attacks, jacks will take any reasonable fly that is presented. Captains watch for "blow ups" of fleeing baitfish to signal a crevalle jack feeding frenzy. Jacks are strong, dogged runners that rarely jump. Most are three to six pounds, but they can be much larger. The world record is 57 pounds, but giants are said to exceed 70 pounds.

Small jacks are common in bays and the surf, larger ones are found around structure in the Gulf and near bridges in big schools. Crevalle jacks of 15 pounds or more travel in smaller schools and are more discriminating. They are fond of rapidly retrieved yellowish streamer patterns. Crevalle jacks do not have sharp teeth and can be handled safely. It is best to grasp them firmly behind the gills with thumb and forefinger. That seems to calm them. Jacks have dark meat that often has parasites, and are not considered good to eat.

Ladyfish

These long slender silvery fish strike flies with enthusiasm. When hooked they make long, fast runs and

Ladyfish caught on flats.

jump repeatedly. Most bay fish are one to two pounds, but those offshore are bigger and may exceed five pounds. Ladyfish are often caught while fishing for redfish or seatrout. They appear ghostlike in the water and are difficult to spot.

Mackerel

There are two species of mackerel that are regularly caught in Texas: Spanish and king. Spanish mackerel travel along the coast, sometimes in huge schools chasing baitfish as they move north in spring. Most are less than five pounds though they have been taken up to eight pounds in Texas. Spanish mackerel are good fighters and like streamer flies, in white and chartreuse, with a fast, scooting retrieve. Fly-fishermen often catch them off jetties in the summer. They are popular for food and sport.

King mackerel are much larger—up to 70 pounds or more. They are toothy and aggressive fish that are regularly caught near offshore oil rigs, but during warm stable weather, when the blue-green water comes near to jetties and beaches, they can be caught in the surf, off piers, and from jetties. A steel leader is a must for king mackerel, and a good idea for Spanish.

Triple Tail

A big strong panfish-looking fish, that is fun to catch, and good to eat. The tripletail's dorsal and anal fins are set far back, above and below its tail giving it a triple tail look. They have an affinity for shade and are most often found around structure such as pilings, buoys, floating weeds, or even floating boards and flotsam. They can sometimes be spotted floating on their sides on the surface as if asleep, "looking like discarded trash bags," as one biologist put it. Tripletail eat baitfish, shrimp, and crabs. When on the surface, tripletail can be cast to, but blind-fishing structure works best. Cast beyond the structure and pause the fly when it comes near. Tripletail are prone to striking a motionless fly.

Tripletail inhabit tropical and sub-tropical waters world wide. Most are in the 2- to 10-pound range but they can get much larger. Forty-pounders have been caught off South Africa, and 30-pounders in Texas.

Saltwater Fly-Fishing

Flats Fly-fishing

Texas coast fishing, and to some extent the fish, is divided into flats, bays, and offshore, with flats by far the most popular venue among fly-fishermen. It is an even bottom contour that defines a flat rather than depth. Flats can vary in depth, but in practice they are considered to be the wadable parts of the bays that are perhaps two feet or less in depth. The best flats water for sight-fishing is about 12 to 15 inches deep. At that depth, a redfish or seatrout's tail will definitely stick out of the water when they feed. Fly-fishermen usually target redfish and seatrout on the flats, but ladyfish, flounder, and black drum are also good possibilities. Jack crevalle, snook and tarpon, and a host of incidental fish can sometimes be taken in open bay water.

Flats fishing is, in large part, sight fishing. One strives to cast a fly, usually a shrimp, crab, or baitfish pattern, a discrete distance ahead of a cruising redfish or seatrout. When the fly lands you must begin stripping immediately before it sinks into the seagrass. Small poppers are fished the same way even though they stay on the surface, because frightened shrimp move quickly often skipping across the surface.

When I fished with Eric he either poled the boat along, let the boat drift across the flats with the wind on a calculated course, or stuck the pole into the mud as an anchor and let the fish come to us—each method worked. He displayed no inclination to wade, and neither of us got our feet wet.

Other captains that I have fished with on the flats prefer to park the boat and wade. Captain Kathy Sparrow explained that she likes to get clients away from the boat so they can concentrate on fishing and not worry about hooking her while casting.

Wading the flats for redfish and seatrout is addictive. It is not something that you can or should do hurriedly, and it seems that you are barely moving until you look back and the boat is hundreds of yards away. The system requires stealth, so you move cautiously and slowly, while keeping a low (bent) profile and watch for tailing or cruising redfish and seatrout to come within casting distance. Whether to wade after them or be still and let them come to you is always a good question.

Discerning the tail of a redfish or seatrout from the omnipresent mullet, that are constantly breaking the surface and imitating game fish, is an acquired art that can never be totally mastered. Even experts such as Chuck Scates, who co-wrote *Fly-fishing the Texas Coast,* readily admits that he, like everyone else, casts to mullet from time to time, but with experience can one significantly reduce their casts to mullet. Texas mullet species, white and striped, have a deeply forked tail. Redfish and seatrout tails are more squarish, and they wave as they swim, while mullet tails tend to quiver. Seatrout tails are darkish green, similar to that of a freshwater rainbow trout, and they are difficult to spot. Redfish tails are golden and lined in blue with a spot, but you can only see that if the light is right. Both fish make wakes as they move, mullet do not. When cursing or in swimming in extremely shallow water, redfish and seatrout may expose part of their dorsal fin in addition to their tail. That is how Captain Scott Sparrow of the Kingfisher Lodge explained it to me, and it helped immensely.

Redfish tail.

Kathy Sparrow putting on stingray guards.

Another reason to wade slowly is stingrays. These otherwise non-aggressive cartilaginous relatives of sharks, that some people catch and eat, can effect a dreadful wound when stepped on. Stingrays lie on the bottom and often bury themselves partially in the mud making them difficult to impossible to see. Stingray guards, made of heavy gauge material like that of bullet proof vests, that fit around one's ankle are available, but most flats fishermen move slowly and shuffle their feet to warn the stingrays of their approach, and the ray moves off. Unfortunately, even veteran flats fishermen can be distracted when fishing, lose their concentration, and make, what was in Captain Scott Sparrow's case, a nearly fatal mistake.

Planting a foot on a stingray's back gives it the necessary leverage to really stab its tail sideways into an ankle or downward onto a foot. Otherwise it cannot bury its stinger like it did to Scott. The stinger passed between his Achilles tendon and ankle bone, it did not go completely through, but came close enough to make an exit wound. The pain was horrible (perhaps half those who are struck go unconscious, and most fall), his muscles began to freeze, and the wound bled profusely. He had to be helped to the boat. Scott was fishing in a tournament and it was a special day for him and his companions. Rather than go in and see a doctor he persevered. After about four hours, the pain stopped and Scott thought the ordeal was over, but it was not.

A far more insidious problem was a bacterial infection known as *Vibro vulnificus*—related to cholera and most commonly associated with eating raw oysters. It is sometimes incorrectly called flesh-eating bacteria (narcotizing facilities), but the symptoms are similar, and *Vibro* has been identified as a causative agent of the real flesh eating bacteria which one can also acquire while wading flats.

Scott's *Vibro* infection was planted by the stinger, so the actual sting was only beginning of his ordeal. Scott's pain tolerance, dedication to his duties, plus an initial misdiagnosis cost him several days of fever, chills, lesions, swelling, and nearly his life before he was properly treated. According to the Center for Disease Control about half the people who contact this infection in the bloodstream eventually die.

This bacteria grows fastest during hot weather in stagnated backwaters. Where there is tidal in and out flow, it does not present so much of a problem. Although it was a stingray that caused Scott's ordeal, it is more commonly contacted by waders with cuts, wounds, or sores on their ankles—same as flesh-eating bacteria which is too horrible to discuss. Suffice it to say stepping on stingrays and wading the flats in hot weather with cuts or open sores on your legs should be avoided.

Flats boat and fly-fishermen.

You should also watch out for snakes on the flats. There are thousands of islands in the bays, some are bushy mangrove affairs, others are grassy, and some are almost devoid of vegetation, but there can be rattlesnakes on any of them. Be cautious when you step from the water and onto dry land when on the flats.

There are numerous places along the Texas coast where you can drive to the shore of a bay, get out and wade. There are many more flats that are accessible by boat. Any shallow drafting boat will get you around the bays and near flats. Jon boats with 15 horsepower motors are often recommended. Negotiating extremely shallow water in and about the flats requires either a modern high-powered flats boat, that when on plane can skim over inches of water, or a sea kayak that requires no launch ramp. Kayaks have recently blossomed in popularity. TPWD has created six marked kayak trails that make it possible to access good bay and flats fishing without fear of getting lost. The trails are at Lighthouse Lakes, Port O'Connor, Mustang Island, Christmas Bay, Armand Bayou, and South Bay. It is also expected that the Texas Parks and Wildlife Department will set aside more and more no-prop zones, where kayaks can enter and high-powered flats boats cannot.

Flats boats have V-shaped tunnel hulls. The four- to six-foot tunnel starts well back from the bow, narrow and shallow at first and widening and deepening towards the stern to form a pocket in front of the motor. Moving water, which adheres to surfaces, goes up into the tunnel and comes out the back about a foot above the water's surface. With the motor trimmed up, the propeller uses the water from the tunnel, and doesn't have to reach the water's surface and stays higher than the bottom of the boat. This allows the boat to go wherever the hull will float which is three inches or so on some. It takes some speed to get that foot of water out the tunnel, so from a standing start it is necessary to get the motor all the way up to the tunnel, turn the boat to the side, and start the boat forward. When a sufficient amount of water comes out through the tunnel the propeller gets traction and the boat jumps up on plane.

Wind and storms are the most prevalent problems for flats fishermen. Wind whips up shallow bays and the mud on the bottom. A sustained strong wind will turn the flats a dirty chocolate color for days. If you insist on fishing under such circumstances the only thing to do is try to find the lee sides of grassy islands where there may be a small amount of relatively clear water where fish will feed, and you can see them. It is not the preferred tactic, but experienced captains may be able to save the day for you.

Texas is a stormy state and the coast is not an exception. Thunderheads with lightning and blinding rain come off the Gulf with alarming rapidity. I was on Aransas Bay with Captain Bill Smith, (now retired from professional guiding), when a black cloud appeared in the distance. Each time I turned to look, which was often, the cloud was twice the size it was on the last look. Then Bill confirmed my most pressing concern—the now-huge group of black storm clouds was directly between us and the harbor, and headed our way. We decided to face it before it got worse. It wasn't long before we were in the storm and the rain was stinging our faces, then it intensified to the point that it was impossible for Bill to see and we had to tie up to a duck blind and wait it out. Lightning, something for which I have great respect, especially on the flats where there is no place to hide, crashed around us. The lightning wasn't severe, by Texas standards, but the rain even impressed Bill. After what seemed like an hour, but was probably only 20 minutes, the storm passed and appeared to dematerialize a few hundred yards away. I think we caught the worst of it at the worst time.

No one should ever go out in a boat, and especially on the Texas coast, without rain gear. On that day I had a heavy, lined raincoat in my bag that was far too warm for a day in the 80s—or so I thought. After taking buckets of water for an extended length of time I was soaked to the skin, even with the jacket, and beginning to feel a bit cool. The term hypothermia even entered my mind. I don't know if the jacket was leaking or water was wicking in somehow. The physics of that rain were surely capable of extraordinary soaking. Probably the former, but whatever the case, it really rains in Texas and you need high-quality rain gear.

Another problem on the flats is high tide. Except under extreme conditions, one or two feet is about all one can expect the tide to vary along the Texas coast, but one foot of water gives redfish and seatrout about twice the area in which to roam, and allows them to grub along the bottom for shrimp and crabs without showing their tails. Blind-casting works, but is nowhere near as productive or fun as sight-fishing. Bill and I were also fighting a high tide that stormy day, and the best redfish came when Bill spotted a mudline while running across the flats. He turned around and I cast to the front of the mud, missed a fish, cast again and got a nice one. Then they were gone and the storm showed up. High tides are to be expected in spring and fall.

Oyster reefs present another shallow-water opportunity for fly-fishing. They are less pleasant to wade on than sand, but exceedingly rich and productive. The entire food chain is present—from algae, small bugs, and shrimp larvae, to crabs, worms, and shrimp, to redfish, seatrout, flounder, black drum and several other fish. Reefs are not so easy to see, and they are consistently overlooked by fly-fishermen.

It doesn't take many high-powered flats boats in a small bay to cause conflict. Etiquette dictates that you do not cut off another boat's drift, do not pull in front of anyone poling or wading a shoreline, and don't go between a boat and the shore if that boat is within a couple hundred yards of the shoreline. It is also dangerous to speed through shallow water along shorelines where waders or kayakers may be concealed behind points and weeds.

Much of this is subjective. On a rough day it is not so critical as on a clear calm day when fish are spooky. Bait-fishermen are concentrating on a smaller area and one less likely to be compromised by another boat, and there are limits on how much shoreline a wading or poling angler can claim. As a general rule, the shallower the water and the calmer the day the greater the separation you should maintain from other boats and fishermen.

Captain Paul Brown, a guide at Redfish Lodge on Copano Bay, says far too many fishermen speed around, or zigzag across, flats looking for fish when they should stop and wade likely water. You may see many fish while running, but few if any of those will take a fly after being spooked. Paul prefers to pick a good stretch of shoreline, park the boat, and wade. He reasons that while you may see only five fish as you wade, you can catch all five, but if you spook 50 with the boat you won't catch any.

Jetty Fly-fishing

Jetties are a convenient but slick alternative to wading and boat fishing. Their great advantage is that fly-fishermen can access deeper water and fish that are more associated with the Gulf than the bay systems, as well as bay species. Bull redfish (the big ones that have left the bays forever), seatrout, large ladyfish, jack crevalle, tarpon, snook, king and Spanish mackerel, and even grouper are commonly or at least sometimes taken off jetties in season in addition to many other species. I have heard of sailfish hooked off South Padre's north jetty, and groupers caught there on poppers.

Jetties are constructed with big rocks, usually granite, which are kept wet and slick by waves and ship wakes. Getting down to the water's edge to landing a fish, especially a big fish like a tarpon, is extremely dangerous or impossible without carbide cleated boots or strap-on sandals like Korkers.

Larry Haines, co-owner of The Shop, a fly shop

one block before the Queen Isabella Memorial Bridge (called the causeway) that connects South Padre Island with Port Isabel and the mainland, suggests using an intermediate sinking line to keep the fly below the waves and debris but not so deep that it hangs in the rocks or allows a hooked fish to immediately get down in them. Three feet is a good depth for jetty fishing.

It is a long and precarious hike out and back on some jetties so it is imperative that you take along everything you need and stay out for a while. Carrying a backpack loaded with food, water, a small gaff (for lip gaffing) fish like mackerel, gloves, and both steel and fluorocarbon leaders are recommended. If there are tarpon about, you will need to carry a 10- to 12-weight outfit, and the standard eight-weight. Stripping baskets are helpful to keep your line out of the crevices which have broken glass and all manner of things you don't want your line to come into contact with. Fly line also has a tendency to become hung on and in the rocks, so line management is an important factor in jetty fishing success.

Watching for baitfish and reading the water is the key. If the tide is creating a strong current you should look for places where baitfish can shield themselves from the flow. Eddies and slack water are likely to hold baitfish and where you find baitfish, you will find predator fish.

Fishing the jetties from a boat can be fun and effective, but requires constant boat management. The boat must be kept near enough to the rocks that you can hit them with a fly, but not so close that you risk being thrown against them. Nor do you want to park in front of jetty fishermen, or run over their lines. This is not an activity for one fisherman. Someone capable and experienced must man the motor at all times, and that motor must not fail. When the water is calm it is possible to cut the engine from time to time, but boat traffic and wind usually won't allow that for long, if at all. Jetty rocks seem to draw boats, and if the engine fails to start, things will get ugly in a hurry. This is doubly true for fishing on the inside or between jetties where wakes keep the water rough, and big ships coming through cause you to have to get out in a hurry—they are much faster that they appear.

Fly-Fishing in the Surf

Fly-fishing in the surf is another option. Merely walking out into the surf and casting is a low percentage tactic. Surf fishing involves reading the water while driving slowly or walking along the beach watching for fish in the wave faces, bird activity, baitfish blow-ups, and shark fins. Surf fishermen watch for shark fins for two reasons. One is for safety, and the other is that when predator fish like mackerel, tarpon, and jack crevalle are feeding on mullet and rain minnows,

sharks are right behind them. Whenever fishing is exceptionally good, there will be many sharks in the area. They will come right up to the shore like killer whales after seals, and are most dangerous when you are out on the second, or (rarely) third, sand bar. Black-tip sharks are the most common along the Texas coast and they are rather shy, but there are also hammer heads, tigers, and bull sharks which are big, bold, and a threat to humans.

Reading the water is a complex, highly technical exercise, like reading the water in a trout stream. Basically, you look for water that holds baitfish, and consequently predator fish. An incoming tide pushes water and baitfish towards the beach and a low tide pulls them out. It is safest to surf fish at high tide because the fish are close to land, and there are no rip currents. Cast at a 45-degree angle, not straight into the waves. Wave action creates sand bars and depressions running parallel with the beach of various lengths. Between these bars are troughs of deeper water called guts. Guts that have an inlet and outlet (much like a pool in a river) fish best.

At high tide, the first, or inner, gut has enough depth to hold fish, at low tide it will be necessary to wade out to the first bar and fish the second gut, which, because Texas beaches are typically shallow, is a long way out. There may be a second bar and third gut, but that is usually not safe for waders. If there are rip or strong side-to-side currents and you step into a hole, you can be swept off your feet and drown. Knowing the water and surf-fishing experience moderates the danger, but type III inflatable life vests are advised for everyone. Anyone can make a mistake, and the ocean is famously unforgiving.

Water color indicates depth. Light green is shallow and dark green is deeper. Deep green holds fish. There are points along the beach that jut out, sometimes subtly, and deep water lies between them. Other places, the wave action has created holes. When the Gulf is calm, water color is more apparent. When it is not, breaking waves indicate bars, and swells indicate guts.

If the surf is not high you can fish from outside the waves from an anchored boat, but you do not want to beach a boat on the Texas coast except in an emergency. A big wave can easily move the boat forward to the point that you cannot push it back in the water, or take it out in the Gulf and leave you stranded.

There are at least as many, and probably more, stingrays in the surf as on the flats. It is imperative to wear stingray guards; stingray proof boots are better. You can also step on lesser electric rays, that look like stingrays except they have fish-like tails. They can provide enough of an electric shock to knock a person down, but not enough to seriously injure anyone. There are also jellyfish, but they are easy to spot and avoid. Larry Haines suggests carrying meat tenderizer in case you are stung, a long-used practice of surf fishermen and surfers.

Outgoing tide is much safer and more productive to fish from the outside with a boat. Fish will be in the second or third gut and waders are not going to reach them. You can drift along watching for the same signs of fish, and if they do not appear, move to another area.

Texas beaches are public highways, provided you reach them by public means which can be roads or ferries. The rules of the road are about the same. Only street legal, licensed vehicles are allowed, and pedestrians (who may not be watching for traffic) have the right of way.

Offshore

In Texas, offshore means from the beach out to the blue water. In that vast area there is a myriad of fish species that will take a fly. Captain Chuck Skates says you can catch anything with flies offshore that you can with conventional tackle. Predator and school fish are most likely, such as Spanish and king mackerel, bonita, barracuda, black fin tuna, and snapper, among many others.

Shrimp boats attract fish when they stop to clean their catch. Fly-fishermen can pull up to them and catch several species. Fly-fishermen also find and catch fish around the offshore oil rigs.

Offshore fishing is not for everyone, it takes time and fuel to get out there, and unless the Gulf is glassy, the ride and stay is going to be somewhat, to extremely, rough. Most offshore fishing is done with large boats and multiple clients that fish on the bottom with bait, but for a price you can go out into the Gulf with captains that will accommodate fly-fishermen.

For serious money, you can go far out into the blue water on boats with staterooms and stay out for days. In addition to what you can catch closer to shore, there are swordfish, marlin, sailfish, tuna, snapper, barracuda and about 500 more species to catch out there.

Captain Smith casting for seatrout under threatening sky.

The Upper Coast

Above: Bolive Peninsula coast.
Upper coast sunrise.

Below: Rollover Pass.
Lower right: Pelicans on pilings.

21

Sabine Lake

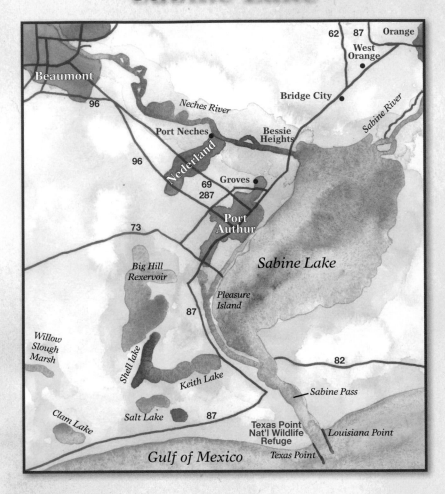

Sabine Lake is a brackish bay, freshest of the Texas bay systems, where most fishermen target redfish, seatrout, and flounder. In its upper reaches, where the water is freshest, largemouth and striped bass, blue catfish, crappie, can be caught alongside redfish, croaker, black drum, and sand trout. The lower portion has all these saltwater species, plus Gulf species, such as Spanish mackerel and lady fish.

Sabine Lake is a dynamic system, it can be all fresh or salty water can come through the pass and move far up into the lake. Heavy flows from Toledo Bend Reservoir on the Sabine River, with flooding on the Neches and Angelina rivers, and other streams can push salt water completely out into the Gulf. When this happens, seatrout escape Sabine Lake's fresh water and congregate out from the pass in the Gulf. In winter, striped bass from the Toledo Bend tailwater are sometimes caught around the jetties during wet years.

Sabine Lake does not lend itself to sight-fishing. From winter through mid-summer the water is turbid, and only in late summer does some green Gulf water with a degree of clarity come into the lake. Should the approach of green water coincide with low flows from the rivers, it can make it to the northern part of the lake, but typically the green water comes only to the northern end of Sabine Pass or the southern part of Sabine Lake.

The beach is a different matter. From Texas Point, near where Sabine Pass meets the Gulf of Mexico, all the way to Port Boliver, slightly north of Galveston, the water is clear in summer.

Unlike other Texas bays, Sabine Lake is an enclosed system that is fed by three major rivers on its north end then opens up into what Jerry Mambretti, the area Ecosystem Leader, likens to a stomach shape, then goes south into Sabine Pass and out into the Gulf. Where the pass meets the Gulf, at Texas and

Flock of roseate spoonbills and swimming alligator near High Island.

Louisiana points, there are jetties on each side that are accessible by boat. Though you can get to these jetties and fish them with a boat, getting out and standing on them is a different matter. Parking a boat against the rocks between the jetties would probably be the last act for that boat, but it is possible from the outside. According to Jerry, anglers do access the jetties from the downwind side of the downwind jetty and climb the rocks with a safety line attached to their boat. The algae-covered rocks are kept wet and slick from ship wakes washing over them, so they are precarious at best, and there is a real danger of being washed off them.

While there is enough room for two ships to pass going opposite directions, the rule for Sabine Pass and the jetties is three ships in, then three out. So, you should not be caught between ships approaching from opposite directions—the worst case scenario. However, if you see one coming, after one passes the other way, there will be two more behind, and you will have to get out of the pass and stay out for a while—then you will have to watch for them coming from the other way.

It is possible to access these jetties on foot, but you have to wait for a low tide and wade a quarter mile through marsh, oyster reefs, and open water. Then you can only go a mile on the slick rocks before the first boat cut. Jerry does not recommend that you get out on the jetties.

The open-water portion of Bessie Heights Marsh, west of the extreme northwestern portion of Sabine Lake, is an especially scenic area with pretty fall foliage and good fly-fishing for redfish. It has year-round clean water that is two to three feet deep, and an abundance of blue crabs for redfish to eat. The redfish from this water are particularly striking with black backs and bright gold sides.

Man-made Pleasure Island, on the east side of the ship channel between it and Port Arthur, provides fishing opportunities. On the south side is a fishing pier and park. On the north end on the lake side is a pocket formed on the south revetment road that is good for trout. On the northern end, summer fishing for big trout early and late is excellent.

Another prime area for fly-fishing is the east end of Sabine Lake—the Louisiana side. This shore is completely undeveloped, and a reciprocal agreement between the states allows Texas fishermen to fish the Louisiana shore, even stand on it. You cannot, however, go back into the bayous without a Louisiana license, and all fish landed in Texas must comply with Texas regulations.

Tarpon are seen periodically in the lake, but the best local bet for them is down the coast at High Island, which is not an island. It is a small town that sits upon a 38-foot-tall salt dome, which is the highest point on the Gulf coast between Mobile, Alabama and the Yucatan Peninsula. Jerry recommends driving through the town of High Island then turning east towards Sea Rim Park. Parts of the beach road were destroyed years ago by Hurricane Jerry so a four-wheel-drive vehicle is required. Tarpon are most numerous from mid-August into September when the menhaden are schooling near shore and big redfish are in their pre-spawn feeding pattern. On calm mornings, tarpon can be seen flashing in the surf, and they come within casting distance.

At the south west end of Sabine Lake is a marshy area with significant open water called Keith Lake. It is excellent water for redfish and seatrout, and great for flounder. The mouth of the Keith Lake Fish Pass is another good spot. On the Keith Lake side of the pass is a significant oyster reef that produces good seatrout fishing. During October and into November, white shrimp move out of the marsh and anglers can do well fishing under the birds. Access to Keith Lake is almost entirely by boat, and in addition to good fishing it affords a sense of seclusion.

Sabine Lake took a direct hit from Hurricane Rita in 2005, and the town of Sabine Pass became instantly famous as the official spot where the hurricane's eye made landfall. Fortunately Rita was not so strong as Katrina, and there is more marsh land between Sabine Lake and the Gulf than there is south of New Orleans. Marsh is resistant to hurricane winds, and massive inflows of salt water and outflows of fresh water are not rare or perilous for Sabine Lake. Structures and boats took a beating, and the resulting pollution closed down commercial oyster fishing, but the sport fishery was largely unaffected.

22

Galveston Bay

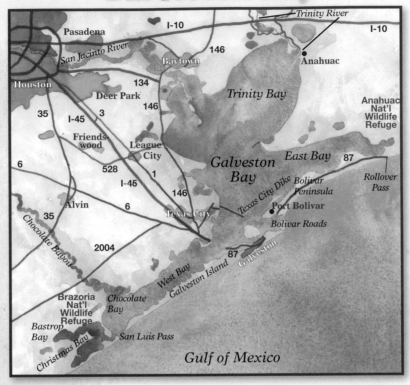

The 600-square-mile Galveston Bay System is the largest of the eight Texas bay systems, and is divided into four major sub-bays: Galveston proper, West, Trinity, and East bays. There are also several smaller bays including Drum, Christmas, Bastrop, and Chocolate bays that are connected to West Bay. There is Dickinson, Dollar, and Tapps bays off Galveston Proper, and an abundance of lakes and bayous of varying size and salinity. Within this massive complex are several dredged channels for ocean-going ships and barges, including the Houston Ship Channel that is about 50 miles long.

The channel was dredged from 40 feet deep and 430 feet wide to 530 feet wide and 45 feet deep in 2005, allowing aframax class tankers, (the world's largest ships), to pass one another in the channel. Previously the channel had to be one way when an aframax came in or went out, seriously slowing shipping.

The Texas City Ship Channel is another main channel, and there are several more, including the ICWW. Within the bay there are flats, shell reefs, spoil islands, the Texas City Dike, and oil and gas wells, with ferries, commercial fishing, pleasure boating, swimming, and fishing all going on at once.

Galveston Bay proper is the hub of shipping activity, and where boaters must be most alert and knowledgeable of nautical procedures and rules. While it is not illegal for sport boats to use the ship channels they should be avoided when possible. It is illegal, and supremely foolish, to impede the progress of commercial shipping. Never stop or anchor in or near a shipping channel. The rule about sailboats having the right of way does not apply under these circumstances, and if a sailboat gets too close to the lee side of a big ship the wind will be blocked and it will be dead in the water. Don't expect a tug with four or five barges or a tanker to make a maneuver to avoid you, there is no place for them to go except the channels, if in fact they see you. There are blind spots of a few hundred to thousands of feet ahead, depending on the type of shipping. Big ships make huge wakes, especially when they must turn to follow a channel, stay as far from them as possible. Five blasts from a ship's whistle means that the pilot is concerned about a dangerous situation. One hopes never to hear this, especially in a small boat.

Big ships are deceptively fast. Like locomotives, their great size makes them seem slow, but they are not. Commercial ships and barges must sustain seven or eight knots to maintain steerage, and are likely to be doing about 15 in the bay. Cutting in front of one could be likened to trying to beat a train at a crossing. Crossing too close behind a ship under power would be a terrifying and, in a small boat, final experience. Wheel wash from the propellers can suck a small boat or even the bow of a barge into the propeller from hundreds of feet away.

Wakes are deceptively far behind ships—five minutes or so. If you don't know that you are in for a surprise. Ship wakes may take the form of large swells or breakers in shallow water near the channels. Rebecca Hensely, Ecosystem Manger of the Galveston system, says that even experienced boaters like those of the Texas Parks and Wildlife Department can get into trouble. Intent on their net sampling near shore, a boat crew either didn't notice that a barge had passed or had forgotten about it. Then about five minutes after the barge passed a five-foot wave caught their boat broadside and nearly capsized it. Fortunately they were in shallow water and no one drowned. That was in the Red Bluff area, south of the Bayport Channel, an especially dangerous location.

The Galveston District of the Army Corps of Engineers recommends that when a wake cannot be avoided that you should point your boat toward it at a 45-degree angle, sit down, and remain calm. I can't imagine being calm in such a circumstance, but what else is there to do? The most amazing statistic I have found regarding Galveston Bay is that there have been no fatal boating accidents since records have been kept. There have been plenty of close calls, mostly at Boliver Roads where there is a two- to three-knot current, three ferries running constantly, ships entering and leaving the Houston and Texas City channels, and all manner of fishing and pleasure boats. It is estimated that within five miles of Galveston Bay there are 80,000 sport boats 16 feet or longer registered.

Despite the complexities of shipping and all the other activity, Galveston Bay is a great place to fish with many attractive features. One is the Texas City Dike, part of Texas City's flood control system, that extends five miles into Galveston Bay with a 600-foot lighted fishing pier at the tip. The pier offers the deepest water for pier fishing in the state, and a chance for Gulf species like tarpon and mackerel in addition to seatrout, redfish, and flounder. There are wadable flats on the north side, and rocks to fish from on the south. However the Texas City Ship Channel runs close to the south shore of the dike and people have been washed off those rocks.

Jim Collins, who works in the White River Fly Shop at Bass Pro Shops' Outdoor World store in Katy (a suburb of Houston), suggests night fishing under the pier's lights for seatrout. He uses a variety of patterns including rattle type Bendbacks, spoon flies, and glass minnow patterns, but Jim has the most confidence in white-and-chartreuse Lead Eye Clousers. Jim considers the Clouser in those colors to be the Galveston Bay System's most effective fly. In addition to piers, it will work on flats, over oyster beds, in the bay, around passes, and off jetties, for seatrout, redfish, flounder, and about any other fish you are likely to encounter in the Galveston Bay System.

There are also service facilities, camping, motel accommodations, and boat ramps on the dike. The Sansom-Yarborough Ramp, located near the end, is a convenient and popular ramp for boaters who wish to get out into the Gulf and fish the rigs. Rebecca Hensley says timing is important here. Wakes from passing ships can change the water level three feet within a minute, and if you don't notice you will drop your boat onto the concrete or prematurely float it off the trailer.

There are more wadable flats along the bay's west shore north of the Dike, and flats to the south of Dollar Point, at Seabrook, and Morgan's Point just south of where the Houston Ship Channel goes inland. Much of this shore is protected from north winds, and fishes well in winter. This is another area in which you should pay attention. Passing ships can pull the water and sediment off the flats and out from under your feet.

Trinity Bay, to the north of Galveston Bay, is lined with flats. Fishermen wade on both sides of the private Houston Light and Power cooling pond spillway on the upper left side of the bay. In winter, the warmer water from the spillway attracts redfish, seatrout, and striped bass. The shore is private and it is a long wade to reach the outflow, so most fishermen go there in boats.

The extreme northern reaches of Trinity Bay are tricky to access. A strong north wind will drive water away from the shallows, and a strong inflow from the Trinity River will make the area deeper and bring in debris. It is constantly changing, and experienced locals and alligators are the major users of the area.

From Anahuac (the official alligator capital of Texas) down to Smith Point, nearly all the east shores of Trinity and Galveston bays, are lined with wadable flats. The Trinity River enters at Anahuac and freshens the water considerably when it is flowing hard. The river's inflow also puts a great deal of silt on the bottom and the footing is not so stable here as it is to the west and south. A strong inflow will sometimes concentrate fish into the northeast corner, or Anahuac Pocket.

Flats continue around Smith Point where East Bay begins, and continue along the marshy area to Anahuac National Wildlife Area on the east end. In the lee of light winds, East Bay can have relatively clear water. Light northwest winds produce relatively clear water along the north shore, and conversely a light southeast wind will clear an area along the Bolivar Peninsula shoreline. The ocean side of the peninsula

Young Anahuac Alligator

is good surf fishing back up to the Sabine Lake area.

Rollover Pass, sometimes called Rollover Fish Pass, is on the far east end of East Bay and links the bay with the Gulf via the small Rollover Bay. The pass was opened in 1955 by the Texas Game and Fish Commission to allow seawater to enter East Bay and stimulate underwater vegetation growth. The pass is 200 feet wide, five feet deep, and 1600 feet long. It is named Rollover because barrels of goods were rolled over the narrow beach between the Gulf and Galveston Bay to avoid Galveston customs, before the pass was opened. It is a popular and productive destination for anglers seeking seatrout, redfish, flounder, Spanish mackerel, black drum, sheepshead, and a variety of other fish. Giant redfish are regularly caught in the surf during September.

Across Boliver Roads is the northern point of Galveston Island and the City of Galveston, which was once the largest and most prosperous city in Texas. That changed suddenly and forever on September 8, 1900 when the most devastating hurricane in US history killed approximately 6000 of the 37, 000 inhabitants. Winds exceeded 120 miles per hour and may have been up to 140 mph (weather instruments of the day were crude, so exact wind speed will never be known). A 15 1/2-foot storm surge washed across the island—its highest point between eight and nine feet. The water carried with it a two-story wall of debris that smashed everything in its path. Bodies were recovered at the rate of 70 per day for at least a month.

Today there is a 17-foot, three-mile sea wall and the entire city has been elevated. Raising the city was done by first raising the surviving structures, then pumping in a sea water and mud slurry under them. When the slurry dried, more was pumped in. It took seven years. Many hurricanes have come and gone since then, including one in 1915 that killed 275 people, but otherwise there has been a comparative minimum of property loss and deaths since the big one in 1900.

The Gulf side of Galveston Island provides surf fishing and general beach activities. The other side is West Bay which has the clearest water in the Galveston System. Jim Collins recommends West Bay and the surrounding area as the best part of the system for fly-fishing. Between Galveston Island and the main-

land is a maze of flats, reefs, bayous, where redfish, seatrout, black drum, flounder, and other fish can be found. There are places where you can drive to the shore, wade out, and catch fish. TPWD is actively renovating the grass flats in the area around the state park, and they have come back nicely. Jim cautions that there are soft bottoms interspersed with hard sand in this area, and for that matter, throughout the bay system. Bird Island Flats, in the extreme south west corner of West Bay, is another excellent fly-fishing spot.

On the southwest end of Galveston Island is San Luis Pass, the largest pass on the Texas coast, through which a huge volume of water, along with bait and predator fish, passes. Seatrout are the primary quarry, but huge redfish and Gulf species such as mackerel and tarpon can also be caught here. Fishing is best on the north side. Wading can be done, but this is a place where you can drown, and someone does about every year. The pass is most dangerous on an outgoing tide. The water's force creates current and whirlpools that are strong enough to suck the sand out from under your feet. Then you fall and get swept out into rough water by a rip tide. Jim says to stay near shore or close to other waders where the bottom is firm and the drop-off gradual, know what the tide is doing, and wear a personal floatation device.

Separated from West Bay by Mud Island is Christmas Bay, a favorite of fly-fishermen. The bay is protected from all sides, surrounded by wadable flats, clear except when the wind blows hard, and accessible from Galveston Island and the mainland. There are places where you can drive to the shore from 3005, aka the Blue Water Highway, wade out, and fish. It also has a kayak path.

Christmas Bay provides good fly-fishing year round, but can fish exceptionally well in winter. It has a maximum depth of about four feet, and is one of the shallower parts of the Galveston System. On sunny winter days its shallow, clear water heats up fast, and fish move in to enjoy the warmth.

On the north side of Christmas Point is Bastrop Bay, a small shallow and protected bay. Bastrop's southernmost pocket has grass flats along the shore where redfish and flounder congregate, and seatrout farther out around the many oyster reefs. Drum Bay, on the south side of Christmas Bay has many oyster reefs. It is productive, but wading is not so convenient as at Christmas Bay.

The Galveston Bay system is the number-one Texas shrimp fishery, so shrimp flies work here as they do all along the coast. There is also a substantial blue-crab fishery. Game fish have the shrimp and crabs, plus baitfish, such as anchovies, silversides, mullet, plus small drum species and croakers. The many oyster reefs supply mud crabs and various other invertebrates. Galveston Bay offers outstanding fishing, but be careful.

The Middle Coast

Top: Wind blown foam pattern and approaching storm on flats.
Left: Backwater off Aransas Bay.
Above: Cruising seatrout.

23

Cedar Lakes

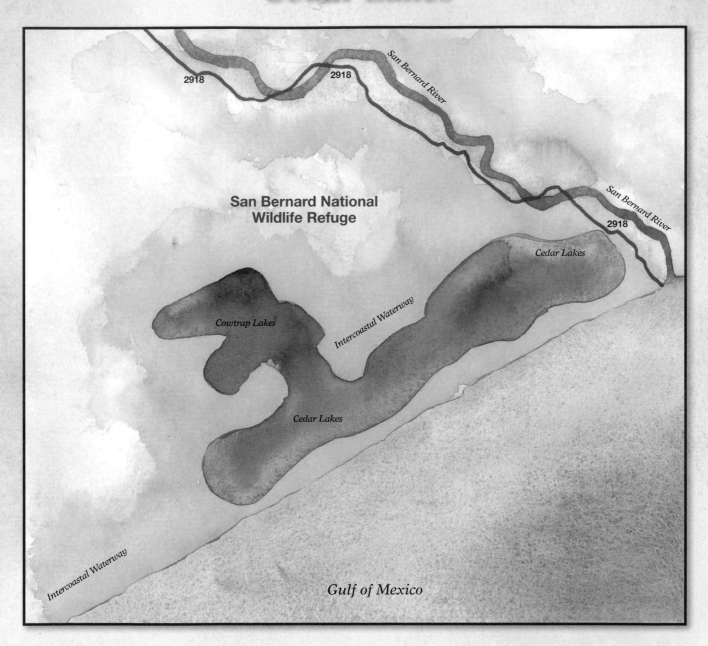

D own the coast from Christmas Bay, and slightly south of Freeport, is the Cedar Lakes area. The Texas Parks and Wildlife Department considers it to be the uppermost point of the middle coast. It is neither a part of Galveston or Matagorda bay systems.

It is not a bay system, but a series of shallow lakes that is thought to be an old bay system that has filled in. The Cedar Lakes are on Gulf side of the Intra Coastal Waterway. On the inland side is the San Bernard Wildlife National Wildlife Refuge. The only accessible water on that side is Cowtrap Lake, a murky lake that holds redfish and a few seatrout and lots of oysters.

The Cedar Lakes are also shallow and murky due to the inflow of fresh water. Its salinity stays at about

Colorful redfish.
Lower right: Choosing a fly for
seatrout on a moonlit night.

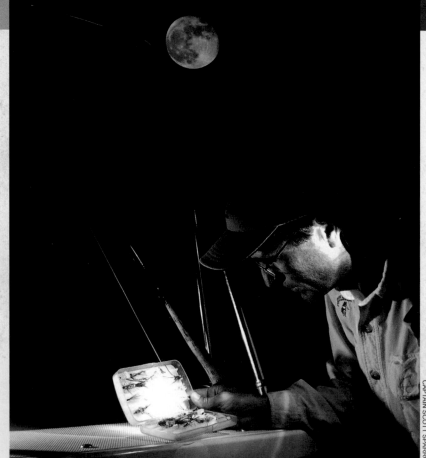

15 to 18 parts per thousand, and
heavy rainfall or increased flow
from the San Bernard River will
turn the small volume lakes to
fresh water. Most of the fresh water comes down the Intracoastal
Waterway. The mouth of the San
Bernard River is constricted and
excess water goes into the ICWW.
Sediment from the Brazos River
that meets the Gulf in Freeport
drifts south and continuously
forces the San Bernard's outlet
down the coast. The silt from
the San Bernard keeps the lakes
turbid and the bottoms soft. Biologist Britt Baumguardner says
that he never steps out of a boat
in Cedar Lakes without hanging
onto the side. Cedar Lakes lack
clear water and a hard bottom,
but has an exceptional population of redfish.

Matagorda Bay

Matagorda Bay, often called West Matagorda, and its sub-bays, East Matagorda, Carancahua Bay, Tres Palacious, Oyster Lake, Keller Bay, Lavaca Bay, and Powderhorn Lake, are heavily influenced by freshwater inflow. Most comes from the Tres Palacious and Colorado rivers. Originally there was no East and West Matagorda bays, but in the early 1900s a channel was dredged across the bay to the Matagorda Peninsula to divert the Colorado towards the Gulf and help alleviate flooding on the lower river. The Colorado was redirected into Matagorda in 1990.

Fly-fishing and wading is mostly done along the inside of the barrier islands, and Matagorda Peninsula where the water is clearer, the bottom more stable, and there is sea grass. This area is sheltered from the prevailing southeast wind and less influenced by the fresh water and silt inflows. There are redfish, seatrout, black drum, flounder, jack crevalle, and the occasional ladyfish. The Gulf side of the barrier

CAPTAIN SCOTT SPARROW

Pale redfish caught in clear water over light sand.

The fresh water provides optimum oyster growth, and there are significant oyster reefs. There is some deeper water around them that makes for good fishing, but biologist Bill Balboa likens wading them to walking on mud mixed with broken glass.

Keller Bay does have some fly-fishing potential on its southwest corner where it is sheltered from the wind and there is sea grass and the water is relatively clear in spring and summer. In winter, when the wind is from the north the mainland side of the bay system becomes the protected side and fishermen catch seatrout at Palacoius off the seawall or by wading out to the oyster areas near shore.

Matagorda Bay is one of the few bays that has a significant recreational fishery for tripletail. These deep-bodied, hard-fighting fish are caught in deeper water around gas and separator platforms, channel markers and other structure where they congregate in late summer. There are some fat snook in the Port O'Connor area as well, and tarpon are sometimes taken in Matagorda Bay.

The westernmost portion of West Matagorda Bay near Pass Cavallo, which divides Matagorda Peninsula and Matagorda Island, and where Saluria Bayou comes out, is known for tarpon. A great volume of water and baitfish are funneled between West Matagorda and Espiritu Santo bays, and the Gulf in this area. Slightly out from Saluria Bayou there is a trough that varies from 25 to 45 feet in depth; perhaps the deepest spot in all of the Texas bays. Pods of tarpon move in and out of the deep water and pass along the island's shore and around the bayou near the old Coast Guard Station at its mouth. There is hard sand from the Mule Slough area to Bayucos Island, and the water is clear. Wading and fly-fishing for tarpon can be good in this area from July to September.

The Matagorda system is rich with shrimp, crabs, and baitfish. There are gulf menhaden, silversides, bay anchovies, striped, white mullet, pinfish, a common and important baitfish that is related to sheepshead and often called "piggy perch," or "piggys," mud minnows, which are a killifish, and crabs. Although Matagorda Bay is the second biggest producer of shrimp on the Texas coast, baitfish-imitating streamers are considered to be the most reliable flies.

islands can be fly-fished in late summer and early fall when the wind dies down, mackerel can be caught in addition to trout and jack crevalle.

Matagorda Bay is known for seatrout, the largest of which are usually found in East Matagorda Bay. During fall and winter they can often be spotted by watching gulls and caught with streamer patterns like those Jim recommended for the Galveston System. The Bay's Matagorda Peninsula shoreline, and the islands between West Matagorda and Espiritu Santo, are wadable and fish well for redfish. Shrimp flies, small Bendback patterns, and shrimp-colored Seaducers are effective here.

The smaller bays and areas adjacent to the mainland are reduced salinity areas where the transition is often freshwater marsh, to brackish, to saltwater marsh. Their turbidity and soft silt and clay bottoms make sight-fishing impossible and wading difficult.

★ 25

San Antonio Bay

S outh of Matagorda Bay is San Antonio bay and its sub-bays, Espiritu Santo, Mesquite, Hynes, and Guadalupe Bays. The bay system is almost completely shielded from the Gulf by Matagorda Island. Its only significant outlet to the Gulf is Pass Cavallo between the Matagorda Peninsula and Matagorda Island, but there are a gauntlet of islands between Espiritu Santo Bay and the pass, which is in West Matagorda Bay, that constrict flow. Most fresh water from the Guadalupe and San Antonio rivers,

which have joined by the time they meet the bay, and the Green Lake/Victoria Ship Channel moves south between the mainland and Matagorda Island. Except for Cedar Bayou which passes little, and sometimes no, water between the bay and Gulf, that water goes into Mesquite Bay then into Aransas Bay and out Aransas Pass. The San Antonio Bay system holds fresh water much longer and is fresher than the other Texas bays, with the exception of Sabine Lake. Fresh water from the Guadalupe River may

The Middle Coast

101

take four or five days to reach the Gulf after it flows into San Antonio Bay.

Matagorda Island is accessible only by boat, or the State Park Ferry from Port O'Connor. The island has no electricity, drinking water, telephone, or concessions. Matagorda offers 38 miles of beachfront and 32 miles of shell-paved roadway that can be used for hiking or biking. There are no vehicles, except for government ones.

The island was once an Air Force Base and at one point used as a bombing range. Now the north end is a state park with some basic amenities such as campsites, cold showers, and a bunkhouse that is open seasonally with a generator and hot showers. The rest of the island is operated by the U S Fish and Wildlife Service as a refuge. Since the Air Force left the island it has been minimally impacted by humans, and is a good place to get away from civilization. Rattlesnakes are common along the coast, and Matagorda Island has the western massasuga rattlesnake which is a plains species and indigenous to northern Missouri and Nebraska. Why they are on Matagorda Island is a mystery. The west side of San Antonio Bay and the north side of Mesquite Bay borders the Aransas National Wildlife Refuge, which is the winter home of the rare whooping cranes.

The refuge is off limits to fishing from October 15 to April 15 when the cranes and other migrating birds are there. When the refuge is open to fishing there are productive wadable flats that can be driven to. During the closure, signs are posted around the refuge's perimeter that warn anglers in boats not to approach sensitive areas.

The group of islands, cuts and bayous between Port O'Connor and Matagorda Island are mostly sand with sea grass and some of the clearest water in the area. The area is known locally as the "Back Bays," and includes Rarwell, Grass and Bayucos islands, Saluria Bayou, Lighthouse Cove, Mule Slough and various other features that are sand dominated. There are soft spots, but much of the Back Bays are solid and wadable, as is the bay side of Matagorda Island itself.

Pringle Lake is well known for fly-fishing. It is protected from east winds by Matagorda Island and north winds by a spit of land called Banderveer Island. Pringle and nearby Contee Power, and South Pass Lakes, Chain of Lakes, Corey Cove, and South Pass are wadable but only accessible with a shallow draft boat. Shoalwater Bay near Seadrift is another clear grassy bay where redfish congregate in fall. It is easily accessible by boat from the mainland at Charlie's Bait Camp. Both Pringle and Shoalwater bays are wadable in some places, and not in others, but they are both good for drift fishing.

Cedar Bayou is a small natural pass between Matagorda Island and San Jose Island. There is not enough head pressure from freshwater inflow to keep it open. It regularly closes, then a storm will open it for a while and then it closes again. A group out of Rockport is campaigning to keep it open. Norman Boyd, Ecosystem Manager for the San Antonio Bay System, says that if Cedar Bayou was made 50 feet wide and three feet deep it would have a positive, but not significant. impact on the bay. If, however, it was made 100 feet wide and ten feet deep, and kept that way (which would be expensive), it would make a measurable difference on the bay system by allowing organisms, water, and fish to pass between the bay and Gulf. Otherwise, Cedar Bayou isn't going to appreciably affect the bay system if it closes.

Like the rest of the coast, redfish and seatrout are the San Antonio Bay's main game fish, but flounder, tarpon, and Florida pompano can also be caught in the area.

As there is no private vehicle traffic on Matagorda Island, the surf side is not so busy as the other barrier islands, and fishing is good. Most fly-fishermen go after mackerel and tarpon in September from boats off shore, but there are plenty of big seatrout to be caught there as well. Otherwise you could ride a bicycle along the coast and sight-fish. Some anglers run their boats into Power Lake and walk across the island to fish the surf.

★ 26

Aransas Bay

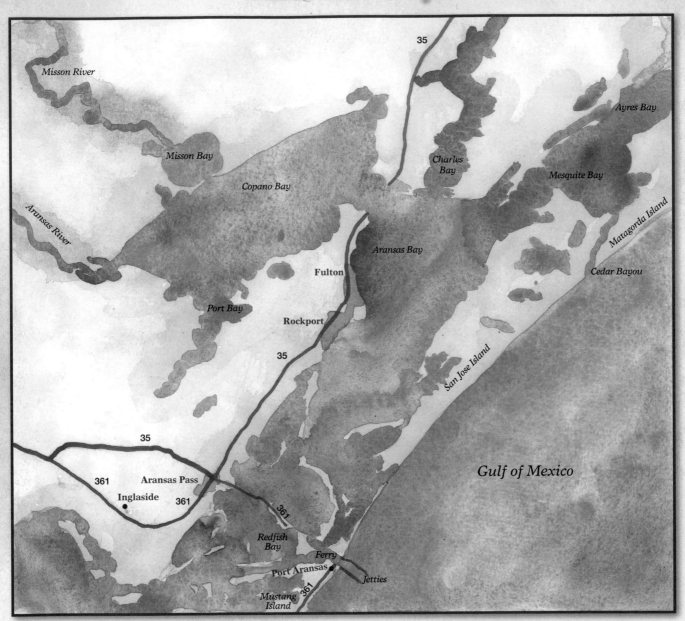

Misson River

Misson Bay

Copano Bay

Aransas River

Port Bay

Fulton

Aransas Bay

Rockport

35

35

361
Aransas Pass

Inglaside

361

Redfish
Bay

Ferry

Port Aransas

Jetties

Mustang
Island

361

35

Charles
Bay

Ayres Bay

Mesquite Bay

Matagorda Island

Cedar Bayou

San Jose Island

Gulf of Mexico

A ransas is the southernmost mid-coast bay system. Its major sub-bay is Copano a shallow bay separated from Aransas by the Lyndon B. Johnson Causeway on Highway 35, which parallels an older bridge that is now a public fishing pier. There is also Mesquite, Carlos, St Charles Bay, and the extremely shallow (about two feet) Mission Bay, which is off Copano Bay. Redfish Bay is divided by Highway 361 which goes from the town of Aransas Pass to Port Aransas. The north side is part of the Aransas Bay System, and the south side belongs in the Corpus Christi Bay System. There are fishable flats and access on both sides of 361 as well as the Aransas Channel on the north side. Highway 361 does not cross to Port Aransas, which is on Mustang Island, but there are free ferries to the island that run 24 hours a day.

Cars in line for ferry to Port Aransas.

Aransas Bay is where the temperate and tropical zones converge. It is the northernmost system with significant turtle grass and mangroves. Turtle grass is the climax seagrass that is valuable to the ecosystem. It is difficult to replenish, and there are no-prop zones to protect it.

Redfish and seatrout are the main species of interest for fly-fishermen, but there are also flounder, jack crevalle, some snook, and a few tarpon. Franklin Delano Roosevelt came there to fish once, and stayed at the venerable Tarpon Inn. The Inn, in operation since 1886, has withstood hurricanes and fires over the years. It is famous for hosting FDR and other celebrities, and for the wall of signed tarpon scales in the lobby. Tarpon were not released in those days, and everyone who caught one could put a scale on the wall and sign it. It is hard to imagine tarpon ever being so plentiful.

Aransas Pass and Port Aransas, which was at one time called Tarpon, was once "the" place to catch tarpon on the Texas coast. People came from all over the world by train, before cars were common, and fished for them around passes that have long ago been closed by shifting sand. From April through October, Arnasas Bay teemed with tarpon. There were so many that on days when the Gulf was rough, guides could take their sports on the bays and catch them.

Older guides around Port Aransas say that as late as the 60s they would not fish Copano Bay for seatrout and redfish because there were too many tarpon. In Mesquite Bay, guides were used to catching a seatrout, redfish, or black drum with every shrimp, and when the action slowed, that meant tarpon were around, and tarpon meant trouble. Such guides have been known to refer to tarpon as "nasty SOBs" because of the way they destroyed trout tackle. One of these veteran guides told Paul Brown that after

enduring about three disastrous tarpon hookups while fishing for redfish and seatrout, you would begin to think of them in that context.

Today, most of the tarpon hooked around the Aransas Bay System are accidental. Paul says that in

Tarpon Inn in the 1930s.

his ten years of guiding in the area he has seen a noticeable increase in tarpon sightings, not only in Copano but also in Arasnas, San Antonio, and Mesquite Bays. They are still not seen so frequently that he and the other guides can target them. Paul recommends keeping a heavy fly rod rigged and ready as the best approach. He says that there are about a dozen calm days during a summer that are perfect for sighting tarpon. All the rest have enough chop on the surface to make spotting them tough. The tarpon are still there and you may still see one, but there is nothing like a "slick off" when the wind subsides and the surface is glassy for spotting a rolling tarpon from a distance. The chances of a visiting angler being there for one of those days are slim compared to the chances of a local fisherman waking up to a perfect day for tarpon fishing.

In Aransas Bay, the back side of San Jose Island from Spaulding Reef and Bight southeast of Carlos

Bay, almost all the way to Port Aransas has a hard sand bottom and, because it is protected from the prevailing southeast wind, clear water. About midway, is Mud Island, which also has good wading and wind protection on its north shore.

There is a long stretch of wadable shoreline, with several small lakes and inlets along San Jose and Mud Island that fish well when the wind is not blowing from the southeast. It begins at the Intracoastal Waterway near Cove Harbor and continues along Turtle Bayou, Talley Island, Trout Bayou, Traylor Island, Big Bayou, Corpus Christi Bayou, and the length of Quarantine Shore to the Lydia Ann Channel. It is mostly hard sandy shell bottom with seatrout, redfish, and flounder.

The entrance to Aransas Pass is also the entrance for ships to the Port of Corpus Christi. The south jetty can be driven to, but you have to boat to the north one, and there is a shuttle service that goes there every hour or so. The channel is relatively narrow and busy, and no place to be in a sport boat when a ship comes in or out.

Paul took me out there in hopes of catching a mackerel, jack crevalle, or bull redfish against the jetty rocks. On the way we were following a sizable boat and crossing its wake was somewhat uncomfortable,

even in the substantial bay/flats boat. Shortly after I began casting, a speck appeared far out in the Gulf. A few casts later the speck was twice the size as it was. The speed at which that big tanker approached the pass was impressive, and I realized that we had been following the pilot boat on the way out. Within 15 minutes of sighting the tanker it was bearing down on us and it was time to go. Paul turned the boat around and when we cleared the pass we went north into Aransas Bay and the tanker went south down the Corpus Christi Ship Channel. The next time I looked, the tanker was barely visible. It was amazing how a ship of that size, even an empty one, as it could have been, could cover so much distance so quickly.

Copano Bay is still good for seatrout, as well as redfish. There are several reefs in the bay and jutting out from the north and south shores. Copano Reef protrudes from the north shore about halfway across the bay and is only one foot under the water. Almost all the south shore, from Redfish Lodge on Rattlesnake Point to the LBJ Causeway, has private lighted piers. The lodge uses stadium lights for their customers who often go out after dinner to fish for seatrout and redfish at night. All this light encourages fish to feed at night, and they seem to be getting used to it.

President Franklin Delano Roosevelt on tarpon fishing trip to Port Aransas in 1937. He caught a four footer.

Redfish Lodge fly-fishing guide Paul Brown scans the flats for tails.

That may mean that they do a bit less daytime feeding, but Copano still fishes well during the day.

The good fly-fishing water on Copano Bay is limited, and if the weather gets bad because of its round shape that water goes bad quickly. The bay is relatively isolated, and if you launch out of the back bay and bad weather catches you, it is a long, rough ride to calmer water. Paul Brown says, at that point you have two choices: put your boat on the trailer and haul it somewhere else, or go home.

You will also face some stiff competition. There are six full-time professional guides who work for Redfish Lodge, all of whom are knowledgeable and effective. On a typical year they fish Copano 60 to 90 days with their clients. Normally, they spend the morning fishing for seatrout, and the afternoons for redfish. They know this bay as well or better than anyone, and you aren't likely to reach the good spots before them.

Redfish Lodge is an upscale establishment that caters to upscale clients and corporations. The lodge occupies all of Rattlesnake point, is gated, and once you are there you will need for nothing. They specialize in two-day, three-night, all-inclusive fishing, hunting, and holiday packages, but also do bird watching. There are many options, and the lodge is capable of working out practically anything you could wish for. Being there is enough. The bay side is hard sand bottom and excellent seatrout fishing. The lagoon side of the peninsula is prime redfish water. A 500-foot lighted fishing pier, with green fish lights in the water, on the lagoon side provides day and night redfishing without getting wet. There is also a pool, tennis court, putting green, tackle and gift shop, billiards, games, and miles of private beach, to name a few of the amenities. Meals are exquisite, with a big breakfast at the lodge, lunch on the water, and dinner prepared by Chef Chris Lee. It is a real treat to be there.

Copano has two sub bays, Port, which Paul considers to be a part of Copano and therefore not a true sub bay, and Mission Bay. Mission is round and extremely shallow, with reefs everywhere, and a mud bottom. It is a tough place to use a motor (Paul calls it a good place for guides to go on their day off), and not good wading.

The Aransas system also includes Mesquite and St. Charles bays. On Mesquite Bay there is the

Early morning at Aransas Harbor.

famous-for-fly-fishing Cedar Bayou Flats that is the first flats fish come to from the Gulf when Cedar Bayou is open and flowing. St. Charles Bay has plenty of good shoreline with good grass beds and is good fly-fishing water. The north and east side is Aransas National Wildlife Refuge, so access is limited from October 15th through April 15th. Paul says alligators are abundant in St. Charles during summer, which adds an element of suspense to wading.

Paul recommends and carries four redfish patterns for the Aransas Bay System: size-2 Lefty's Deceiver in a cockroach pattern with a squirrel-tail collar, instead of bucktail. Number two is a gold spoon fly, three a size-6 cork or sponge popper with a red and white body with gold or white tinsel for hackle, and four is a Seaducer on a size-2 hook.

For seatrout he likes big white Deceivers, with a little blue or green, in 2 and 2/0. Sometimes they want the big one and other times they like the smaller version. Seaducers in the same sizes, with white red or green, Clousers in the same size from 2 to 2/0 are good for fishing holes. Paul likes bead eyes for the smaller ones and lead eyes for the larger flies. He uses a leader of up to 14 feet, so he can land a heavy fly as far from the fish as possible to avoid spooking the fish with the splash, while keeping the line a discreet distance—the heavier the fly the longer the leader. With a 14-foot leader he can throw the fly 7 feet past the fish with the line also 7 feet from the fish. A lighter fly will require less cushion—the heavier the fly the longer the leader. The shortest leader Paul will use is 9 feet, and he likes stiff mono because the wind knots are easier to pick out.

Paul also carries offshore baitfish patterns such as a Woolhead Mullet, small (for salt water) Bunker (baitfish) flies, and small mackerel and shad patterns on light hooks to fish the shallow inshore water for jack crevalle.

The Lower Coast

Right: Lower Laguna Madre redfish.
Below: Houses along the Intracoastal Waterway.

Left; Kathy Sparrow holding a sizable seatrout.
Right: Captain Scott Sparrow with a ladyfish from the Intracoastal Waterway.

⭐ 27

Corpus Christi Bay

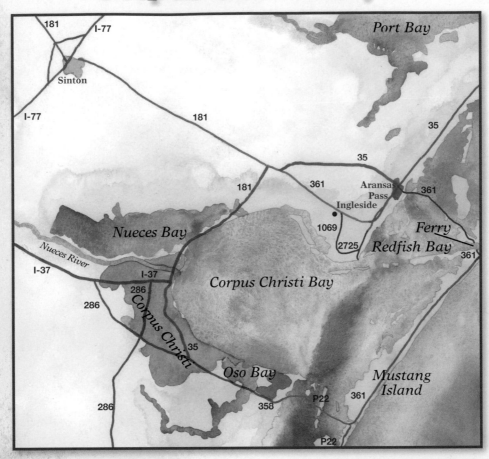

The Corpus Christi Bay System extends from the south side of Redfish Bay to a point between Demit Island and Mustang Island near the Corpus Christi Naval Air Station and north of the John F. Kennedy Causeway that runs from Flour Bluff to Padre Island. Nueces Bay where the Nueces River enters, and Oso Bay that is fed by Oso Creek provide most of the freshwater inflow.

Wading in Corpus Christi Bay is done, for the most part, on the south side of Highway 361 that cuts across Redfish Bay and the Shamrock Cove area between Mustang and Shamrock Islands. The flats along the 361 Causeway are accessible by car, and there are plenty of places to park. Shamrock Cove is primarily a boat-to area, but there is a road in the Wilson's Cut area from which you can wade the sea-grass flats. There is turtle grass in this area on both sides of the causeway, and no prop zones are interspersed, so kayaking is an excellent way to fish this area and the back side of Mustang Island.

Corpus Christi Bay is deep for a Texas bay. A good portion of it is between ten and fifteen feet, even close to the shoreline. It has an uncommon variety of fish species including traditional bay, offshore, and tropical species. The Corpus Christi Channel holds flounder and croaker during the winter months and though approachable, the channel areas are usually murky and not great for fly-fishing.

Good fly-fishing is limited in Corpus Christi Bay. There are piers and shore fishing at Indian Point near Portland on the north side of the bay. Oso Fishing Pier near University Heights on the Corpus Christi Bay also has some shore fishing. The Mustang Island side of the Intracoastal Waterway on both sides of Fish Pass has wadable shoreline as well.

Other than Aransas Pass and some wash-over areas, there were no connections between Corpus Christi Bay and the Gulf until the Packery Channel opened in 2005. It allows recreational boats, but not commercial shipping access, to the Gulf and jetties where tarpon and snook may be caught as they are at Aransas Pass.

Upper Laguna Madre

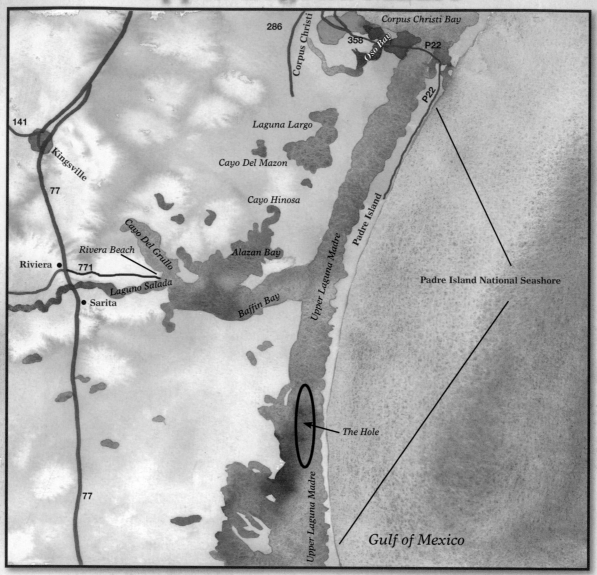

South of Corpus Christi Bay is the Upper Laguna Madre. It is separated from the Lower Laguna Madre by the "land cut," a 22-mile-long section of the Intracoastal Waterway built in the 40s. The land cut runs through dry land by "The Hole" which is the deepest portion of an extremely shallow part of Upper Laguna Madre that was once a shallow flat. In 1919, a hurricane washed sand from Padre Island across the flat and separated the Upper and Lower Lagunas. After the storm, it was only possible for fish to pass from the Upper Laguna and into the Hole when the water level was high. Fish that entered the Hole in spring on high tides were then cut off when the water level was

tides lowered in summer. Salt concentrations would continue to rise through evaporation and eventually reach lethal levels. Now fish can escape the Hole via channels from the Land Cut, and boats can pass between the lagunas.

The Upper Laguna is bordered by Padre Island National Sea Shore, the longest remaining stretch of undeveloped barrier island in the world, on the west and private nearly undeveloped shoreline on the east. From Corpus Christi down to Port Mansfield, about 50% of the mainland shore is either King or Kenedy ranch property. The rest is parts of other large ranches or small private parcels.

Richard King and Miffin Kenedy, founders of these two giant ranches, were steamboat captains that transported troops and supplies on the Rio Grande River for the United States during the Mexican War. They become partners in King, Kenedy and Company and dominated trade on the Rio Grande for nearly two decades. They both amassed large fortunes and bought land near and along the Texas coast. Now the King Ranch is a huge conglomerate, rated number 175 of the 500 biggest Texas companies. It has various and widespread interests in addition to its 825,000-acre ranch with its cattle and energy businesses. The 400,000-acre Kenedy Ranch, originally called La Parra, lies mostly to the south of the King Ranch. It is half owned by a foundation, and half by a Texas bank. Kenedy Ranch also has cattle and energy operations, and what is said to be the largest remaining stretch of native coastal prairie habitat on the Texas coast. There are access points between Kingsville and Sarita, along Cayo Del Grullo a northern sub bay of Baffin Bay, at Riviera Beach, and at county road 1145 on Baffin Bay, on the east side of Highway 77. Otherwise, from the Corpus Christi area to Fred Stone Park at Port Mansfield the coastline is private and as undeveloped as Texas coastline can be. Highway 77 abruptly ended at Sarita, which was named for Sarita Kenedy—the last of the Kenedys, until it was extended to Brownsville in the 40's. There are occasional signs of the cattle and energy businesses, but no condos, private residences, or hotels like rest of the Texas coast. Plenty of people fish the Upper Laguna System, but on a slow day you will get a very real feeling of isolation, and according to Ecosystem Manager Kyle Spiller, it is good to have a cell phone for emergencies because it is unlikely that you will find anyone on shore to help.

The national seashore is on North Padre Island which is separated from South Padre Island by the Port Mansfield Channel or East Cut as it is sometimes called. The island and park can be accessed by car via the John F. Kennedy Causeway from Corpus Christi. The causeway turns into Park Road 22 which dead ends at Malaquite Beach. From there, with four-wheel-drive you can drive and camp for another 63 miles down the beach to the Mansfield Channel (where the Spanish Galleons were found).

Tarpon, mackerel, seatrout, and redfish in addition to various other Gulf species can be caught in the surf. Do not drive far from the hard sand at the beach because if you get stuck you have a problem. Not only are there no facilities down the beach, but if your vehicle gets buried to the point that the park employees cannot free it with one of their SUVs, you will have to call a wrecker from Corpus Christi. That will be expensive. For vehicles stuck 30 miles or so down the beach, the bill will be about $1000.

It is illegal to use personal ATVs (the park employees have them) anywhere in the park, or to drive your car into the dunes or onto the Laguna's mud flats, which is begging to get stuck anyway. You can park on the beach side where the island is narrow and walk across the island to the Laguna and fish flats that would otherwise take a long boat ride to reach. There will be sharp grass and some rattlesnakes along the way, but serious anglers do it regularly.

Baffin Bay, the major sub bay of the Upper Laguna Madre, has a history of producing the biggest seatrout in Texas. It lies on the west side of the Laguna, between Point of Rocks and Point Penascal.

Point of Rocks is named for its serpula reefs and rocky outcroppings that are the product of ancient serpula worms that lived, died, and accumulated in the area when the water was fresher. The area is also called "the badlands" and it is well known for wrecking lower units. Point of Rocks is a hotspot for big seatrout that move in when the sun warms the mud bottom, but it's not a place to speed through if you are unfamiliar with the area. Fluorocarbon leaders are recommended here because of the abrasive rock-like features.

There are other such rocky spots in Baffin Bay, notably around Kleberg Point, and in Alazan Bay to the north. These are hard-bottom, wadable areas, but the footing is uneven. If the water is deep enough, anglers can pull up their motors and drift or move through them using trolling motors to steer. Of course, the shoreline itself is private, but you can wade without trespassing.

On the south side of Baffin Bay at Point Penascal there is a unique and extensive reef system of beach rock that runs 10 miles down and along the shoreline. Sea trout hold against and near the rocks. There are some redfish there as well, but it is primarily sea trout territory. The rocks can be fished by wading along the shoreline, drifting offshore, or maneuvering along and among them with a trolling motor.

Upper Laguna Madre is a legendary seatrout fishery, and most of the fishermen there are targeting them. Redfish are second in popularity. Snook and tarpon are seen occasionally, but not in numbers large enough to warrant targeting them. There is an extraordinary population of black drum though, and a high percentage of the commercial catch landed in Texas comes from the Laguna.

There is not so much freshwater inflow in the Upper Laguna as in the northern bay systems, so the water is much clearer and better suited for sight-fishing. Most of the water is shallow, weedy, and rich with game fish. Fly-fishermen can catch fish anywhere along the Texas coast, but the Upper Laguna Madre is a fly-fishing jewel.

★ 29

Lower Laguna Madre

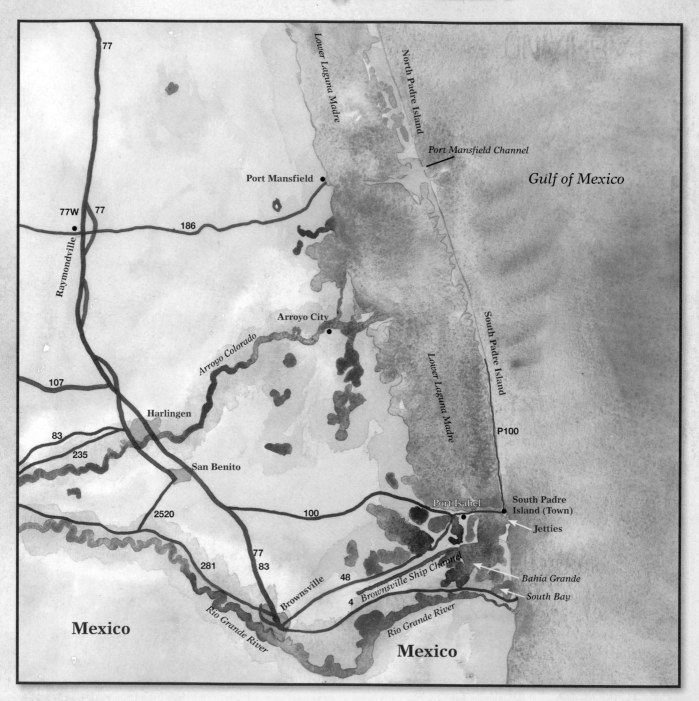

On the south side of the Land Cut is the Lower Laguna Madre—the shallowest bay on the Texas coast. As with the Upper Laguna its shallows are ideal for seagrass. Together the two Lagunas have about 30% of all the Texas seagrass.

Turtle, shoal, and manatee grass is abundant in Lower Laguna Madre. Shoal grass, a thin-bladed species that is common along the Texas coast, is desirable for fish habitat, but a nuisance for fly-fishermen. It attaches itself to flies and line loops, and whatever else

112   *Texas Blue-Ribbon Fly-Fishing*

it comes in contact with, then when a fish comes into range, you can't make a good cast because of it. Attempting to remove the grass usually spooks the fish, and that fish spooks all the others in the area. Stripping baskets are recommended to keep line out of the grass and avoid this cycle.

Other sea grasses have thicker blades and aren't so annoying, but when a fish makes a long run, as redfish do, across the flat, and you don't get the rod tip up quickly, the line will slice under the grass and all the species will accumulate on your line where it enters the water. There can be pounds of grass clinging to the line, holding it to the surface, restricting your control and enjoyment of the fish. If you can reach the accumulation it is possible to grab and remove it, otherwise it will steadily move down the line, toward and finally, to the fish.

Seagrass, though it is sometimes a bother, provides habitat, food, and security and is the basis on which the Laguna's ecosystem is formed. Pinfish and mullet, two primary forage species of the Lower Laguna and the other bay systems, eat algae from the grass blades, shrimp spawn and grow in it, young sea trout and redfish hide and feed in it, and older ones forage in and around it.

Lower Laguna Madre has the clearest water on the Texas coast. Seagrass helps keep the Laguna's water clear by stabilizing the bottom sediments. The bay's shallow water keeps wind from making high waves that stir up sediments and make the water murky. Even in high wind, parts of the Lower Laguna Madre will remain fishable. Casting will be a challenge, but the water will be clear when the same conditions on other bays would make for tough fishing.

The east shore of the Lower Laguna borders South Padre Island, which begins south of the Port Mansfield Channel. This side of the Laguna is much different from the west side. There are fewer weeds, much less mud, and a collar of hard sand around it that varies in width from narrow to wide from the middle section on north. The hard sand is as wide as a parking lot in places and fish can be seen at great distances in the clear water. There are no large concentrations of shrimp on the east side for podding redfish to team-up on. Feeding fish tend to cruise singly or in small groups or three or four looking for crabs, worms, and small croaker (piggy perch). Sea trout are inclined to focus on small fish, but redfish hunt for crabs and worms. Lug worms dig u-shaped burrows that are easily visible in the clear water, and lie in them, head at one end taking in nutrients from the water and the tail at the other. Crabs use these burrows for cover and redfish can root into the hole and suck up both the crab and the worm. Black drum and sheepshead do the same thing.

Redfish may be seen in large groups on the east side, but they are most likely staging for the spawn, or socializing rather than feeding. Ladyfish also frequent the east side sand flats.

South Padre Island is uninhabited for about 20 miles from the Mansfield Channel, south to where the paved road begins and development starts. There, the island changes abruptly from uninhabited beach to towering hotels, condos, expensive beach homes, and a mass of T-shirt shops and restaurants. The town of South Padre Island is famous for crowds of spring breakers. This is not a place to come in March unless you are young, or feel young, and up for a non-stop party. Otherwise, the town is busy all year—more so in summer.

As with the upper island, it is legal to drive on the beach, but not on the dunes. The south jetty at the Port Mansfield Channel can be reached by four-wheel-drive vehicle from the town. The island has some narrow washover sections that may be inundated during high tides or in stormy weather or high surf. It is not a place to be driving when the weather is bad. At low tide it is possible to get along the beach without four-wheel-drive in places, but if you intend to go any distance beyond the pavement, two wheel drive will not do. Several miles up the beach from the end of the pavement, clothing becomes unofficially optional.

Padre Island is connected to the mainland by the spectacular 2.37-mile Queen Isabella Memorial Bridge that is know as the "causeway." In September 15, 2001 a tugboat veered off course at 2:30 in the morning and slammed four loaded barges into the bridge. The collision brought down two 80-foot sections immediately and another fell later. Several vehicles plunged off the causeway and 80 feet down to the water. Eight people died, and the bridge was renamed "Memorial" for them. Measures, including warning lights every 500 feet that flash if a fiber optic cable running the length of the bridge is severed, and railroad-like mechanical arms that drop to stop cars, were installed to prevent another such tragedy.

The causeway was completed in 1971, replacing the old Queen Isabella Causeway. The old causeway has been breeched to allow boat traffic to pass, and is now crumbling and has been fenced off from the mainland side. On the island side, a remnant of it is a fishing pier that can be accessed for a fee.

The uppermost part of Lower Laguna Madre is Rincon de San Jose, a small pocket on the northwest corner that locals call Gladys' Hole or the Northwest Pocket. The pocket is a highly productive lagoon, and when the water level is up you can get a boat to some smaller lagoons farther inland called the back lakes. Captain Scott Sparrow recommends fishing the three entrances to those back lakes, that fish use to move between the pocket and the lakes.

From the pocket, down to Port Mansfield, the shoreline is straight and has few features with no prominent inlets or lagoons, but is good fishing. Slightly north of Port Mansfield, on the west side of the Intracoastal Waterway is an area called Redfish

Bay (not the Aransas sub-bay). Randy Blankenship the Lower Laguna Ecosystem Manager, says that it is more of an area rather than a true sub-bay, because there is no real definition of its parameters. Its major distinction is its deeper water—up to 8 feet or so, depending on tides. It tends to be rough, and is considered to be a good place for spin fishing, and not as good for fly-fishing as the Laguna's shallower parts.

Fred Stone Park at Port Mansfield is the first public access south of Riviera Beach on the Upper Laguna Madre. At Port Mansfield, there are fishing piers, boat launching and supplies. The northern part of Lower Laguna Madre is easily reached by boat from Port Mansfield, and you can also quickly get out to the Gulf via the channel. Local captains often take clients out for bluewater fishing at the oil rigs, or to fish off the coast of Padre Island when the Gulf is calm. South of Port Mansfield there are productive shallow tertiary lagoons, and sloughs along the coast for many miles. The area around Green Hill, Chubby, and Mullet islands receive fresh water from the "floodway," where water from the Rio Grande Valley is diverted toward the Laguna and away from population centers. Normally this is a trickle, but when a hurricane dumps heavy rain it is a torrent. It, and the original Arroyo Colorado channel's fresh water and seagrass, provides perfect habitat for shrimp and blue crabs to spawn and grow, and consequently redfish are abundant in and around the area's many sloughs, islands, and small lagoons.

Between Port Mansfield and the mouth of the Arroyo Colorado Cutoff, the Intracoastal Waterway runs near the west shore and dredge spoil islands have partially isolated some of the bay shore. One such area is called Peyton's Bay by locals. This vast area of open flats is roughly the area south of the floodway and old arroyo channel outlets to a few miles north of where the Cutoff comes into the bay. Peyton's Bay receives fresh water from the floodway and the old channel, has luxuriant seagrass beds, a firm bottom for wading, and is rich with shrimp and blue crabs. Redfish are concentrated in this area and schools of them can be found feeding on the shrimp in spring. When the shrimp move out, the redfish turn to crabs. During summer when the water level is low, few boats can get in, and it is almost impossible to fish with a spinning outfit because of the shallow water and thick shoal grass, but floating poppers are fun to fish on these flats and are also effective in and near the nearby ICWW.

Along this section of the Intracoastal Waterway there are several small houses built on pilings over the water. These are old leases, and no more are being issued. If a hurricane blows one of these houses away it can only be rebuilt if two pilings are still standing, and if it is not replaced within two years, the lease is retired forever.

South of Peyton's Bay is the Mud Hole, a small, shallow, and extremely rich lagoon about one half mile north of where the Arroyo Colorado Cutoff comes into the bay. The Arroyo Colorado is an ancient channel of the Rio Grande that begins near Mission and flows east into the Lower Laguna Madre. It is the Laguna's largest source of fresh water. The cutoff channel has been dredged to make an inland waterway to the Port of Harlingen, and to carry flood water out to the bay. The original channel meanderers into a complex of shallow lagoons, arroyos, and islands and was not straight or deep enough for commercial navigation. The cutoff also allows quick access to the good flats along the Laguna's middle coast, that otherwise would require a substantial boat ride from launch points at South Padre Island, Port Isabella, or Port Mansfield. There is a public boat ramp at Adolph Thomae Jr. County Park, between Arroyo City and the Arroyo's mouth.

Nearly all the homes in Arroyo City are on the Arroyo. It is a fishing community and not a bustling touristy place. Kathy and Scott Sparrow live about four miles up the Arroyo from the bay and Kingfisher Inn is a mile farther. Scott grew up in south Texas and has known the Laguna all his life. Kathy is from upstate New York. She is also a captain - one of the few women to become one - with her own flats boat, but has since retired to just fishing. Scott also takes clients on birding trips to the nearby Laguna Atascosa National Wildlife Refuge. The 45,000 acre refuge is the largest protected area of natural habitat in the lower Rio Grande Valley.

Kingfisher Inn, now owned by Randall Cawlfield, and his wife Lydia, (Captain Scott still guides there) is open year round and fly fishing is all the fishing they do. You are welcome to stay there if you wish to spin fish, but they will hand you off to another local guide. You may also bring your own boat and they will work with you. It is a flexible operation. The lodge itself sits on the bank of the Arroyo, and has units that can accommodate three and five guests. Guests may fish the Arroyo at night, where the Inn's underwater fish lights attract seatrout, redfish, and snook from spring through early winter.

About a half mile inside the Arroyo's mouth there is a channel on the south leading to a shallow lagoon called Parker Lake, or Lake X. It has a hard, wadable bottom, few weeds, and a great deal of algae. Spinning does not work here, but like Peyton's Bay, a weedless popper will produce big redfish in spring and fall when water level is high enough for them to enter and for boats to navigate. South of the Arroyo's mouth there are several islands, shallow coves, and mudflats, that are non navigable except when the water level is up. Lying slightly south of the Arroyo's mouth is Horse Island, which affords good wade

Glassy water on Lower Laguna Madre flats.

fishing on its south side. The island is part of the Laguna Atascosa National Wildlife Refuge and can be driven to, and fishing is legal. At nearby Rattlesnake Island there is a productive channel between it and Yucca Island that is informally called Rattlesnake Lagoon. Maps are notoriously inaccurate for this area because it is so shallow. Only a few inches of water will dramatically change the islands' and lagoons' shorelines, and that happens with every substantial storm.

The shoreline between Horse and Rattlesnake islands, and El Realito Bay, offers an array of super shallow flats that can only be accessed in spring and fall. Immediately to the south of this area is El Realito Bay, a small sub-bay that locals call Cullen Bay because of the Cullen's landmark ranch house that stands on the southern peninsula. Across El Realito Peninsula, to the south is Little El Realito Bay. This shallow shoreline has good wade fishing between Stover Cove and Stover Point. Maps may indicate that you can park along Bayside Drive to fish, but like Horse Island this is contained within the refuge and you cannot. The first public car and fishing access down from the Arroyo is at Holly Beach in Port Isabel.

South of Holly Beach along Highway 100 there are good flats, but as development increases there are fewer placed to access the water.

South Bay, the southernmost part of the Lower Laguna, is in the Laguna's only major sub-bay. It is a beautiful shallow bay that is ringed by black mangroves, with extensive oyster reefs, and is a great place to fish. South Bay is close to South Padre Island and Port Isabella and all the activity associated with that area, but has a feeling of isolation. It was once the southern outlet of Lower Laguna Madre. Water moved through the bay at a rate sufficient to keep the Boca Chica Pass open to the Gulf, and allow boats into the bay. When the Brownsville Ship Channel was dredged, the spoil was dumped along the edge of the channel and restricted its outlet, Boca Chica Pass, to the point that flow diminished and the pass closed. It now stays closed except when hurricanes open it, and South Bay can only be accessed by boat from the north. Due to its unique habitat, the Bay was designated the South Bay Coastal Preserve in 1988. Currently there are no special regulations for the area, and with signs and brochures TPWD strives to encourage minimal impact.

Queen Isabella Memorial Bridge with South Padre Island in distance.

The Rio Grande estuary is the northernmost known reproduction and nursery area for snook, and they are more common in the Lower Laguna Madre than in any other Texas bay system. Normally, the river is about 25 or 30 yards wide and five to six feet deep where it meets the Gulf. Boats that manage to get over the bars and into the estuary can run up the river 46 miles to the rock weir in Brownsville.

In February 2001, the Rio Grande ceased to flow over its bar and into the Gulf. The estuary reopened from July through November of that year then closed again until increased rainfall in the river's watershed opened it in November of 2002. This had some effect on the snook, but it is unclear exactly what that was. At best it disrupted the snook, and other fish, from feeding on gulf menhaden, striped mullet, white shrimp, and Atlantic croaker in the estuary, at worst, two-year classes were lost.

Snook and tarpon in the one- to four-foot range inhabit South Bay and the Laguna during the warmer months. When the water cools, snook head for deeper water around the Brazos Santiago Pass between South Padre and Brazos Island, up the Rio Grande, or into the Brownsville Ship Channel between the Laguna and the mouth of the Rio Grande. Where tar-

pon go is not certain, but they probably move offshore to deeper water or down the Mexican coast.

Both the north jetty at the southern tip of South Padre Island and the south jetty across the pass are excellent fishing. For snook and tarpon they are considered the best in Texas. The north jetty is inside Isla Blanca Park. There is a five-dollar fee to enter that drops to two dollars at five PM. In the summer, fishing doesn't get good until after five so there is no point in paying the additional three dollars. Easy access makes the north jetty a busy place. Most people are fishing with bait for whatever they can catch. Snook are found about where the waves on the Gulf side start. A red-and-white Clouser is a good fly for them. For tarpon you must go at least half way out, and probably farther. The first half of the jetty is crowded anyway, and going out half way gets you some casting room and a better selection of rocks to stand on. It is recommended that you wear cleated boots as the rocks are slick and unforgiving. Either bring a flashlight or be sure and allow time to get back before darkness sets in. Negotiating the uneven rocks is one thing in daylight and quite another after dark.

The south jetty is less accessible consequently much less crowded. Reaching it requires a drive around the Brownsville Ship Channel to Brownsville and then out to Boca Chica State Park via Highway 4, where you then drive north on the beach for several miles.

Every three to five years a serious cold front makes it down to the Lower Laguna Madre. When this happens, the north wind blows water south, down the bay and out the Brazos Santiago Pass. As the flats cool, fish seeking warmer water tend to follow the flow out to the Gulf. When water moving out from the bay meets the south-flowing Gulf water, an eddy is produced on the outside of the south jetty. Redfish, seatrout and black drum from the bay amass in great numbers in the eddy, and fishermen congregate with them. Under these circumstances fish are vulnerable and there is a potential to take fish in numbers that would not otherwise be possible. TPWD is considering future closures under such circumstances. It happened in 1983, twice in 1989, in 1997, and again in 2005.

In January, the water is low, clear and cold. Redfish are sluggish and shrimp are not available on the flats, so they feed on baitfish and crabs. They are looking down and are reluctant to come to the surface or go out of their way to chase flies. By March, the water has warmed and brown shrimp have grown, and moved into the seagrass to spawn. Redfish begin to pod and tail together, driving shrimp to the surface, which attracts birds. Topwater flies and poppers are productive in this period, but the redfish are not

Kathy Sparrow, Diane Hicks, and typical flats red drum.

Author with fat snook that took a red and white Clouser.

selective so they will go for about anything that is well presented. This is the easiest time to catch redfish on the flats.

As summer approaches, the Laguna's level drops with the falling tides, and the water warms. Redfish feed as small groups or individuals on shrimp that are fewer and more scattered. Scott recommends sight-fishing to single fish or small groups with weedless foam-bodied VIP Poppers. He ties them in pink,

yellow, and orange early in the day and switches to sub-surface flies later if the fish seem spooky. Scott uses his Mother's Day Fly, a shrimp imitation, when he sees fish coming for, then rejecting the popper. Shoal grass is thick in many places around the Lower Laguna, so if fish keep going for poppers, he stays with them, because of the weedless advantage they present and because they are so much fun to use.

In fall, the water level rises again and the white shrimp move into the west side of the Laguna to spawn in winter. This causes the fish to begin podding again and bird activity increases. This pattern is usually not so dramatic as in the spring, but topwater flies are good till December. Spoon flies are good attractors and productive in fall when the water is high and sometimes murky.

Big seatrout are available year round in the Lower Laguna Madre, but because of their coloration that closely matches the bottom it helps to have low, clear water and no wind to see them. Scott uses the same flies at the same times for seatrout as he does for redfish. Like redfish they are not selective, and a good presentation will usually draw a strike.

Coming to Texas

Everyone knows Texas is big. Know-it-alls, and Alaskans, delight in pointing out that Texas is less than half the size of Alaska, but that fact is of little consolation to those who must travel around this state. Texas is 790 miles long and 660 miles wide and contains the country's most extensive road system. With few exceptions, fishing in Texas involves considerable driving. Even if you fly to your destination, you are still likely to have a long drive to the water. It is a short (by Texas standards) drive from the Corpus Christi airport to the Aransas Bay flats, and you can fish some good water near Austin, but otherwise count on driving.

Texas roads are wide, well maintained, and mostly straight. Where safe and prudent, drivers will pull to the road shoulder and let others pass, a considerate phenomenon I have rarely seen elsewhere. You will not see many pokey drivers here. Texans are unwilling to spend any more time than necessary on the road. You can get old driving around this state.

Destinations always seem to be about five or eight hours apart, or more, so you get plenty of time to look around and think. In spring, the roadsides are alive with bluebonnets (the state flower), Indian paintbrush, and a wide variety of other wildflowers. Texas has more wildflower species than any other state.

Highway 118 in west Texas' Davis Mountains.

Bright red Indian blanket and yellow coreopsis wildflowers.

Finally, do not even dream of driving to Texas during summer in a car that is undependable. Breakdowns in 100-degree weather are positively life threatening. Bring good tires and a sturdy air conditioner. Refrigeration technology makes Texas livable, without it the Texas population would be about 90% less.

Floodwater

Much of Texas is relatively flat and storm water tends to spread out rather than run down canyons and steep-sided valleys where it is more contained. Flood water

Blue bonnets, the Texas state flower.

Metropolitan freeways are another story. They are flat-out unrestricted races, or parking lots. Timing is important. Don't get involved with the freeways around rush hour, which begins early and lasts late. Even during off peak times, wrecks or construction can bring you to a complete and extended halt any time of the day or night.

Phlox, a common Texas wildflower.

spills over river banks into a myriad of small channels and gullies and suddenly overwhelms the countless low-water crossings around the state. People routinely bet their lives by driving into the water at flooded crossings. Since 1994, about 15 people a year lost that bet. It is the number one cause of weather-related deaths in Texas.

It only takes two feet of swift water to sweep a vehicle off a bridge, and depth is difficult to determine. Compounding the problem, the roadbeds of some crossings are uneven and depth can vary substantially from one section to the next. Video of spectacular rescues (and near rescues) are a television news staple in Texas.

Texas Weather

The southernmost point of Texas is only 180 miles north of the Tropic of Cancer, where the tropics begin. Winter rarely visits southern Texas, but Corpus Christi had an official white Christmas in 2005, and freezing weather does sometimes make it all the way down to Lower Laguna Madre and Brownsville. These unusual cold fronts wreak havoc on fish, wildlife, plants, and the locals. Winter can be surprisingly cold, and warm, in Texas, but it is normally pleasant by most standards, except in the Panhandle where the temperature once dropped to -23 degrees.

Spring comes early to Texas. February is usually mild, and by March the sun is warm. Days with sustained sunshine can easily reach 80 degrees, but it can also be freezing. Generally, things are about a month ahead of the southern Midwest and like the Midwest, spring weather changes from idyllic to terrifying in a matter of minutes.

Texas' close proximity to moisture and unstable air masses from the tropics, Pacific Ocean, and Gulf of Mexico is conducive to hurricanes, tornados, lightning, softball-sized hail, flooding rain and damaging straight winds. Texas is a distant number two in lightning strikes, behind Florida. About eight people die from lightning strikes each year, but the state's size skews that statistic.

Spring is a marvelous time to be in Texas, and a productive time to fish if your timing is good.

Wind blown foam pattern and approaching storm on flats.

Guadalupe National Park.

Planning a Texas fishing trip more than a day or two out is always a gamble, and the odds of having your plans dashed by fierce storms and raging brown water are highest in spring. You can hedge your bet and appreciably improve the odds by allowing more time for your trip (rivers go down as quickly as they go up) and being flexible.

There is hot, and there is Texas hot. The highest temperature ever recorded in Texas was 120 degrees in 1936, which is one degree less than North Dakota's all-time high. Summer comes sooner, gets hotter, and stays longer in Texas. Average summer temperatures are bearable, but average anything is not the norm in Texas. Expect hot sunny weather, stifling humidity, and low water in summer, but be prepared for anything—including a flood.

Due to the oppressive heat and lack of productivity, fishermen tend to avoid Texas reservoirs during mid-day in summer, but river fish feed periodically in the heat, and saltwater fish like it. On a river you may find shade from time to time, but not on the coast. In summer, late spring, or early fall you must be prepared for scorching sun.

When summer's heat finally moderates in late September or October, Texans come out of their air-conditioned houses in droves. Outdoor festivals featuring music, food, beer, wine, history, art, theater, and ethnic themes, and others, take place between the end of the hot and beginning of the cold (for Texas) weather. Fall has a reputation for more stable weather than spring, but it doesn't seem to work out that way as often as it should. When the strong cold fronts meet the Texas heat and humidity, storms develop. Like spring, fall is a great time to fish in Texas, but, also like spring, there will be some storms.

Don't Mess with These Texans

Texas has a major market share of things that bite and sting—both animal and plant—but is rightly famous for its rattlesnakes. Western diamondbacks, the largest and most abundant species, live throughout the state in varying concentrations, except in far eastern Texas. Western massasauga, pigmy, and timber rattlesnakes are found in eastern Texas. Timber rattlers, sometimes called canebrakes, are the only species as large as the diamondback. They are dangerous but secretive and not so aggressive as diamondbacks. The other species are desert massasauga, mottled rock, banded rock, black tail, Mojave, pigmy, and prairie rattlesnakes. Diamondbacks are far more likely to be encountered in Texas than any other rattlesnake.

In East Texas swamps, western cottonmouths are common and a real danger. Cottonmouths, or water moccasins, are aggressive, stubby, big—up to six feet—and capable of biting underwater. Moccasins swim high in the water—unlike water snakes, with which they are often confused—usually with only their heads above the surface.

There are three copperhead species, the southern which is in east Texas, the broadbanded found in central and west Texas, and the Trans-Pecos copperhead that inhabits areas around springs in the southern part of the Trans-Pecos range. Copperheads bite many people, but they are not likely to kill anyone.

It's sometimes said that coral snakes, found in eastern Texas, are more of a threat than rattlesnakes because their poison is more powerful. Coral snakes do have more potent poison, but they are smaller than diamondback rattlesnakes and can't deliver as much poison as effectively. Coral snakes have small fixed fangs and must hang on at least briefly to inject a meaningful amount of poison. They do not have to chew the venom into their victim, but if given the chance they will. Coral snakes' venom injection system is more useful for small lizards, amphibians, and other snakes than for people. Humans are unlikely to allow a snake to hang on any length of time and certainly won't hold still while a snake chews on them. Remember the adage, "red and yellow will kill a fellow." Milk snakes, which live in the same area, look much like them but

Big Texas gator.

black separates the red and yellow. If red touches yellow you are seeing a coral snake.

Big diamondbacks hold massive reservoirs of poison and can inject it in an instant with their retractable fangs. They can kill you. If you encounter one of these snakes leave them be and they will not be a problem. All snakes have their place in nature. The great majority of snake bites are a result of people trying to kill a snake. Watch where you put your feet and hands, avoid brush piles, abandoned dwellings, walking along rock ledges, and over rock piles. Two or three people die of a snakebite each year in Texas, but 5-7 die of insect bites.

Alligators

Alligators have made a big comeback after becoming rare in the 60s. Texas began protecting them in 1969 and they were listed as endangered in 1973. The

Bee hive in west Texas.

Warning at rest stop on Hwy 77 south of Kingsville.

alligator population recovered, and in 1985 they were taken off the list.

Young alligators chirp, and older ones make a bellow that sounds like a chainsaw trying to start. All sizes hiss as a warning. Alligators do not perceive humans as food, but that does not go for pets. Small dogs are sometimes eaten by them, although it is a rare occurrence in Texas.

Alligators are naturally afraid of humans, but mothers will defend their nests and young. Certain

Serious thorns along Brazos River.

individuals can be aggressive, usually as a result of being fed by humans, and are referred to as "rogue" gators. Do not bother, feed, attempt to handle, walk near the water's edge with pets (especially without having them on a leash), swim around alligators (particularly at night), and never allow small children to be close to alligator-inhabited shoreline.

Scorpions

Texas has 18 scorpion species, none of which are considered deadly. The most common is the striped back scorpion—the only species that is found in all parts of Texas. Scorpions live under rocks, boards, in dead vegetation, fallen logs, and houses. They are commonly found in attics, and sometimes move into living areas when the attics become too hot. There are no substantiated deaths attributed to this species. The sting, on par with a bee or wasp sting, causes only local pain

Rattlesnake coiled, rattling, and ready to strike.

and swelling, but allergic reactions are a possibility that will require immediate medical care.

Fire Ants

Fire ants are potentially life threatening, and always unpleasant. There are native species, but the red ones from South America are the most aggressive. Fire ants live all over the south and in Texas, except for a few areas out west where there is not enough rainfall to support them. Fire ants are mostly red, but that is not where they got their name. They bite and inject poison which stings, and to which some people are deathly allergic. First they latch onto your skin with barbed mandibles then sting repeatedly with their other end in a circular motion. Fire ants are extraordinarily aggressive, and will come after you if you annoy them. Watch for the mounds of granulated earth they make, and do not disturb them unless you want to do battle. If you poke a stick at them they will climb it to get at you.

There is No Place Like Texas

Texas has an unparalleled diversity of climate, topography, and culture. There are mountains, deserts, swamps, brush land, and seacoast contained within the state's 172 million acres. Texas shares portions of the West, Great Plains, and South with New Mexico, Oklahoma, Arkansas, and Louisiana. The Rio Grande River defines an 889-mile border with a similar landscape and culture with Mexico. Texas climate varies from western temperate in the panhandle to subtropical in the south, moist in the east, and arid in the west, with blends between.

The varied climate zones and land characteristics produce a spectacular assortment of wildlife. Texas has at least 215 freshwater fish species, and there are 540 species in the Gulf of Mexico, most of which can be caught on or near the Texas coast. There are also 165 species of mammals, and 213 reptile and amphibian species, of which 15 are venomous snakes, and many unusual species including armadillos and three species of horned lizards (aka horny toads) that can puff up and shoot blood from their eyes.

Foundation of house that was moved farther back from the beach due to erosion.

DIANE HICKS

124

Whooping cranes in Aransas National Wildlife Refuge.

Mountain lions live mostly in West Texas, but the Texas Parks and Wildlife Department (TPWD) has records of their occurrence in every county in the state except for the northern panhandle ones. Ocelots and jaguarundis inhabit the state's southern portions. Jaguars once roamed Texas, but there are none presently living and breeding in Texas or anywhere in the United States, so far as anyone knows. Jaguars do reside in northern Mexico, and there are occasional sightings north of the border. Margays were once found here, but haven't officially been seen since 1850, so you probably won't see one.

Whitetail deer are thick enough to be a hazard in Texas. Early morning and late evening when fishermen are likely to be out are the most dangerous times. Deer hunting is a way of life here.

Six-hundred-plus bird species regularly breed, winter, nest in, or migrate through Texas—more than in any other state. Whooping cranes winter on the Texas coast at the Aransas National Wildlife Refuge, near Rockport, and the only place you are likely to see a Tamaulipis crow in the United States is at the Brownsville dump. All serious birders must, at some point, come to Texas.

Serious fly-fishermen should also come to Texas. This state has an established fly-fishing culture, opportunities that exist nowhere else, and plenty of room. Despite all the possibilities, and perhaps due in part to its "desert image," Texas remains one of the less "discovered" fly-fishing destinations. There is a conspicuous lack of pressure here. Longtime Texans may take issue with this because Texas is surely more crowded than in the past, but out of state visitors (y'all) will almost certainly feel a sense of space.

Peccary.

Flies for Texas

Freshwater Flies

Miss Prissy

Peck's Popper (1)

Peck's Popper (2)

Peck's Popper

Conehead Rubber Bugger

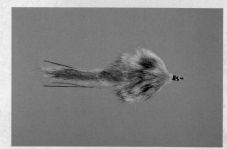

Rob's Lake Fork Leech

Cypert's Mylar Minnow, White

Madame X

Lead Eye Clouser

Lead Eye Clouser, red/white

Rob's Swamp Rabbit

Rob's IC Fly

LIGON Bream Killer, brown

Rob's WITH Bugger

Turk's Tarantula

Charlie Boy Hopper

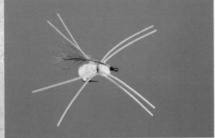

LIGON Bream Killer, chartreuse

Rob's Sili Shad

Cypert's Mylar Minnow, chartreuse

Lead Eye Clouser, gray/white

Action Angler Trout Flies
Tied by Chris Jackson

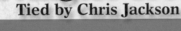

BH Zug Bug

BH Pheasant Tail Nymph

San Juan Worm

Drowned Trico Spinner

Damsel Fly Nymph

Elk Hair Caddis

Trout Portion of Guadalupe River

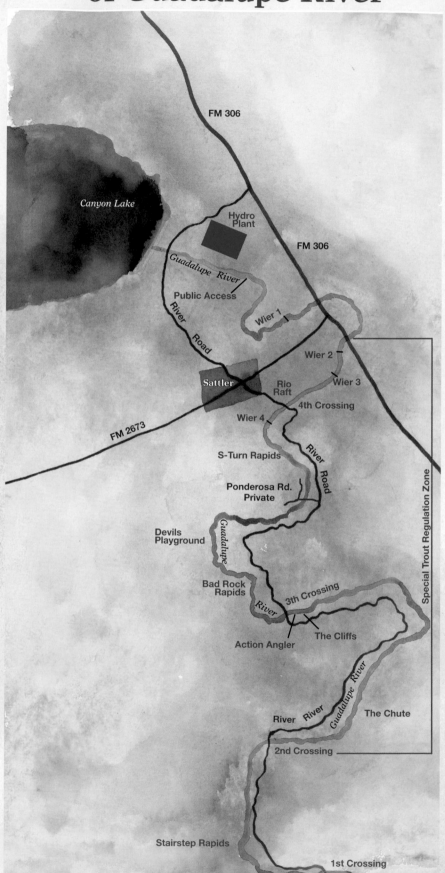

Canyon Lake

FM 306

Hydro Plant

FM 306

Guadalupe River

Public Access

Wier 1

Wier 2

Wier 3

River Road

Sattler

Rio Raft

4th Crossing

Wier 4

FM 2673

S-Turn Rapids

River Road

Ponderosa Rd. Private

Special Trout Regulation Zone

Devils Playground

Guadalupe

Bad Rock Rapids

River

3th Crossing

Action Angler

The Cliffs

Guadalupe River

River River

The Chute

2nd Crossing

Stairstep Rapids

1st Crossing

BH RL Hare's Ear

Hackle Wing PMD

Action Midge

Parachute Hopper

Hackle Wing BWO

Texas Blue-Ribbon Fly-Fishing

CII Olive Krystal Bugger

Prince Nymph

Zebra Midge

Bass Pro Shops/Offshore Angler Saltwater Flies

Skinny Water Minnow, Umpqua

Chernobyl Crab, Umpqua

Cave's Wobbler, Umpqua

Kwan's Bead Chain, Umpqua

Chernobyl Redfish, Umpqua

Bigeye Bendback, Umpqua

Bonefish Slider

Swimming Shrimp

Super Swimming Shrimp

Chernobyl Crab

Fur Shrimp

Deceiver, green/white

Rainy's CB Bubble-Head Bronze/Gold

Rainy's CB In-Shore Popper blue/white

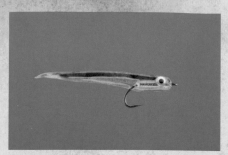

Gummy Minnow, green

Drum Popper, copper

Gold Spoon

Drum Popper, red/white

Cowen's Mullett

Lead Eye Clouser

Mini Crystal Popper, blue/white

Tarpon Bunny, yellow

Tarpon Bunny, orange

Big Eye Tarpon Fly, red grizzly

Cockroach

Texas Blue-Ribbon Fly-Fishing

Lower Laguna Madre Flies

Larry Haines' Tarpon Bunny

Larry Haines' Mae West

Larry Haines' Tarpon Bunny

Larry Haines' Lite Brite Minnow

Larry Haines' Krystal Shrimp

Tom Kilgore's Thousand Dollar Deciever

Capt. Skipper Ray's Deerhair Mullet

*Capt. Skipper Ray's
Bunny Tail Seaducer*

Capt. Scott Sparrow's Mother's Day Fly

Capt. Scott Sparrow's Kingfisher Spoon

Capt. Scott Sparrow's VIP Popper

Bud Rowland's Número Uno (1)

Bud Rowland's Número Uno (2)

Flies for Texas

Texas Resources

Texas Blue Ribbon Contacts

Texas

Texas Parks and Wildlife Department
4200 Smith School Road
Austin, TX 78744
512 - 389 - 4800 • 800 - 792 - 1112
www.tpwd.state.tx.us

Caddo Lake

Food / Lodging/ Guide Services
Shady Glade Resort
449 Cypress Drive
Uncertain, TX 75661
903-789-3295 • 877 - Go Caddo
www.shadygladeresort.com

Area Information
Marshall Chamber of Commerce
P.O. Box 520
Marshall, TX 75671
903 - 935 - 7868 • 800 - 953 - 7868
www.marshalltxchamber.com

Area Fly Shop
White River Fly Shop
Bass Pro Shops/Outdoor World
100 Bass Pro Drive
Bosier City, LA 71111
318 - 549 - 8800

Lake Fork

Guide Service
Robert C. Woodruff
Woodruff Guide Service
3371 N. FM 14
Quitman, TX 75783
903 - 967 - 2665
www.flyfishingfork.com
E-mail: WGSFlyFish@aol.com
East Texas Lakes, Mountain Fork River, OK

Area Fly Shops
Jones Creek - Orvis Dealer
2301 S. Broadway, Suite A7
Tyler, TX 75701
903 - 526 - FISH
E-mail: jonick@spyderinternet.com

Backcountry: Fly-fishing, Camping, Ski, Travel
Southeast Crossing Shopping Center
3320 Troup Highway, Suite 125
Tyler, TX 75701
903 - 593 - 4602
E-Mail: jrverde@gower.net

Possum Kingdom Lake

Dean Heffner
Heffner Guide and Tour Service
940 - 779 - 2597
325 Butler Point Road
Graford, TX 76449
E-mail: fav7734@aceweb.com

Brazos River

Guide Service
Andy Moreau
Brazos River Fly-fishing
817 - 569 - 9389
www.BrazosRiverFlyfishing.com

Canoe Rental - Lodging
The Outpost - Dick's Place
P.O. Box 5408
Laguna Park, TX 76644
254 - 622 - 8364
www.dickscanoes.com

Hill Country Fly-fishing Guides

Bill Higdon
In The Hills Fishing Excursions
1854 Ponderosa Dr.
Canyon Lake, TX 78132
830 - 964 - 5565 • 830 - 708 -5423
www.inthehillsfishing.com
Guadalupe, Llano, San Marcos, Blanco,
Pedernales, and Colorado Rivers

The Guides of Texas
Marcus Rodriguez
512 - 665 - 3261

Johnny Quiroz II
512 - 557 - 6397
www.guidesoftexas.com
All Hill Country Rivers

Alvin Dedeaux Fly-fishing
712 Nowotny Lane
Austin, TX 78704
512 - 663 - 7945
alvindedeaux.com

Kevin Stubbs
Expedition Outfitters
210-602-9284
kevin@msn.com

Joey Lin
Far Out Fishing Trips, J L Travel, Inc.
P.O. Box 907
Austin, TX 78767
888 - 795 - FISH (3474)
www.faroutfishingtrips.com
San Marcos, Colorado, Llano, and Medina Rivers

Kelly Watson
Texas River Bass
512 - 590 - 4458
www.texasriverbass.com
Blanco, San Marcos, Llano, Colorado Rivers

Llano River
Bed & Breakfast - Guide Service - Casting Instruction

Raye Carrington on the Llano
8603 Lower Willow Creek Road
Mason, TX 76856
325 - 347 - 3474 • 866 - 605 - 3100
www.rayecarrington.com

Canoe Kayak Rental - Shuttle
Kendall Hemphill
Rock Bottom Canoe Company
P.O. Box 1600
205 Westmoreland St.
Mason, TX 76856
325 - 347 - 6440
Jeep@verizon.net

Colorado River / Austin
Hotel - Restaurant - Meeting Rooms - Canoe & Kayak Rental
Holiday Inn
Austin - TOWNLAKE Hotel
20 North IH 35
Austin, TX 78701
512 - 472 - 8211

Area Information & Attractions
Austin Convention & Visitors Bureau
209 East 6th Street

Austin, TX 78701
512 - 474 - 5171 • 866 - GO-AUSTIN
www.austintexas.org

Lady Bird Johnson Wildflower Center
4801 La Crosse Avenue
Austin, TX 78739
512 - 292 - 4100
www.wildflower.org

Area Fly Shops

Sportsman's Finest
12434 Bee Cave Road (FM2244)
Austin, TX 78738
512 - 263 - 1888

Cabella's
15570 IH 35
Buda, TX 78610
512 - 295 - 1100

Guadalupe River
Fly Shops
Action Angler and Outdoor Center
9751 River Road @ The Third Crossing Bridge
New Braunfels, TX 78132
830 - 964 - 3166
www.actionangler.net

Gruene Outfitters
1629 Hunter Road
New Braunfels, TX 78130
830 - 625 - 4440 • 888 - 477 - 3474
www.grueneoutfitters.com

Lodging
Gruene Mansion Inn
1275 Gruene Road
New Braunfels, TX 78130
830 - 629 - 2641
www.gruenemansioninn.com

The Cliffs
9751 River Road
New Braunfels, TX 78132
830 - 964 - 4008
www.the-cliffs.com

San Marcos River
Area Information
San Marcos Convention & Visitors Bureau
202 North CM Allen Parkway
San Marcos, TX 78667
512 - 393 - 5900 • 888 - 200 - 5620
www.sanmarcostexas.com/tourism

Devils River
Area Information
Sonora, Texas Chamber of Commerce
205 Highway 277 North, Suite B
Sonora, TX 76950
325 - 387 - 2880

Guide Service
Gerald Bailey
830 - 395 - 2266

Lodging - Camping
Devils River State Natural Area
HC 01, Box 513
Del Rio, TX 78840
830 - 395 - 2133

Best Western Sonora Inn
270 Highway 277 North
Sonora, TX 76950
325 - 387 - 9111 • 877 - 937 - 9111

Bakers Crossing Campground
Comstock, TX 78837
432 - 292 - 4305

Additional Hill Country
Fly Shops

Hill Country Outfitters
115 East Main Street
Fredericksburg, TX 78624
830 - 997 - 3761 • 800 - 672 - 3303
www.hillcountryoutfitters.com

Big Thicket / Village Creek
Eastex Canoe Trails
1698 Business Hwy 96 South
Silsbee, TX 77656
www.texascanoetrips.com

Texas Coast
Lodging - Guide Service
Kingfisher Inn
36911 Marshall Hutts Road
Arroyo City/Rio Hondo, TX 78583
956 - 371 - 8801
www.kingfisherinn@lagunamadre.net

Redfish Lodge on Copano Bay
P.O. Box 2295
Rockport, TX 78381
800 - 392 - 9324
www.redfishlodge.com

Lodging
Tarpon Inn
200 East Cotter Avenue
Port Aransas, TX 78373
361 - 749 - 5555
www.thetarponinn.com

Best Western Rose Garden Inn
845 North Expressway
Brownsville, TX 78520
956 - 546 - 5501 • 800 - 528 - 1234

Fly-fishing Captains
Paul Brown
Redfish Lodge
800 - 392 - 9324

Eric Glass
The South Texas Fly-fishing Company
Box 3745
South Padre Island, TX 78597
956 - 761 - 2878
www.captainericglass.com

Scott Sparrow
Kingfisher Inn
956 - 748 - 4366
kingfisher@lagunamadre.net

Coast Fly Shops
The Shop
318 Queen Isabella Boulevard
Port Isabel, TX 78578
956 - 367 - 2337
saltyflyshop.com

Coastal Information
Beaumont Convention & Visitors Bureau
P.O. Box 3827
Beaumont, Texas 77704
409 - 880 - 3749 • 800 - 392 4401
www.beaumontcvb.com

Brownsville Convention & Visitors Bureau
P.O. Box 4697
Brownsville, TX 78523
956 -546 - 3721 • 800 - 626 - 2639
www.brownsville.org

Galveston Island Convention & Visitors Bureau
2504 Church Street
Galveston, TX 77550
409 - 763 - 6564 • 888 - GAL-ISLE
www.galvestontourism.com

Port Aransas Chamber of Commerce
Convention & Visitors Bureau
Ann Vaughn, Executive Director
403 West Cotter
Port Aransas, TX 78373
361 - 749 - 5919 • 800 - 452 - 6278
www.portaransas.org
Info@portaransas.org

South Padre Island Convention & Visitors Bureau
7355 Padre Boulevard
South Padre Island, TX 78597
956 - 761 -3005 • 800 - 767 - 2373
www.sopadre.com

Metropolitan Fly Shops

Dallas - Ft. Worth

White River Fly Shop
Bass Pro Shops - Outdoor World
2501 Bass Pro Drive
Grapevine, TX 76051
972 - 724 - 2018

Blue Drake Outfitters
Inwood Village
5370 West Lovers Lane
Suite 320
Dallas, TX 75209
214 - 350 - 4665
www.bluedrake.com

Orvis Arlington
3901 Arlington Highlands Blvd., Ste. 101
Arlington, TX 76018
817-465-5800

Orvis Dallas
8300 Preston Road
Suite 300
Dallas, TX 75225
214 - 265 - 1600

Cabella's
12901 Cabella Drive
Ft. Worth, TX 76177

White River Fly Shop
Outdoor World-Bass Pro Shops
5001 Bass Pro Drive
Garland, TX 75043
469-221-2600

Tail Waters Fly Fishing Co.
2416 McKinney Ave.
Dallas, TX 75201
214-219-2500 • 888-824-5420
www.tailwatersflyfishing.com

Houston

White River Fly Shop
Bass Pro Shops - Outdoor World
5000 Katy Mills Circle
Suite 415
Katy, TX 77494
281 - 644 - 2200

Orvis Houston
5848 Westheimer Road
Houston, TX 77057
713 - 783 - 2111

White River Fly Shop
Outdoor World-Bass Pro Shops
1000 Bass Pro Drive
Pearland, TX 77584
713-770-5100

San Antonio

Hill Country Outfitters
18030 US Highway 281 North
Suite 108
210 - 491 - 4416
San Antonio, TX 78237
www.hillcountryoutfitters.com

Sportsmans Warehouse
1911 North Loop 1604 East
San Antonio, TX 78259
210 - 494 - 5505

Sportsmans Warehouse
8203 S H 151 Suite 104
San Antonio, TX 78245
210 - 509 - 4100

Tacklebox Outfitters
6330 North New Braunfels
San Antonio, TX 78209
210 - 821 - 5806

Amarillo

River Fields
2465 IH 40 West
Amarillo, TX 79109
806 - 351 - 0980
www.riverfields.com

Top Notch Outfitters
2617 Wolflin Village Street
Amarillo, TX 79109
806 - 353 - 9468

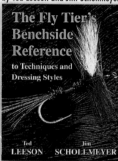